# Education for Civic Engagement in Democracy

## Service Learning and Other Promising Practices

Edited by Sheilah Mann
and John J. Patrick

The ERIC Clearinghouse for Social Studies/Social Science Education and the Adjunct ERIC Clearinghouse on Service Learning in Association with the Task Force on Civic Education of the American Political Science Association

## Ordering Information

This publication is available from:
ERIC Clearinghouse for Social Studies/Social Science Education
Indiana University
2805 East Tenth Street, Suite 120
Bloomington, Indiana, U.S.A. 47408-2698
Toll-free Telephone:     (800) 266-3815
Telephone:               (812) 855-3838
Fax:                     (812) 855-0455
Electronic Mail:         <ericso@indiana.edu>
World Wide Web:          <http://www.indiana.edu/~ssdc/eric_chess.htm>

ISBN 0-941339-50-5

This publication is also available from:
   National Service-Learning Clearinghouse
   University of Minnesota
   R460 Vo Tech Ed Bldg.
   1954 Buford Avenue
   St. Paul, Minnesota 55108
   Toll-free Telephone: (800) 808-7378
   Fax: (612) 625-6277
   Electronic Mail: <serve@tc.umn.ed>
   World Wide Web: <http://umn.edu/~serve>

This publication was developed and published in 2000 by the ERIC Clearing-house for Social Studies/Social Science Education (ERIC/ChESS) at the Social Studies Development Center (SSDC) of Indiana University, with support from the Adjunct ERIC Clearinghouse for Service Learning at the National Service-Learning Clearinghouse (NSLC), University of Minnesota. The NSLC is funded by the Corporation for National Service under contract number 98CAMN0001.

This project has been funded at least in part with federal funds from the U.S. Department of Education under contract number ED-99-CO-0016. The content of this publication does not necessarily reflect the views or policies of the U.S. Department of Education nor does mention of trade names, commercial products, or organizations imply endorsement by the U.S. Government.

Support was also provided for the development and distribution of this publication by the Task Force on Civic Education of the American Political Science Association.

ERIC, Educational Resources Information Center, is an information system within the U.S. Department of Education.

# Contents

# Preface

The essays and references in this special ERIC publication address the problem of the disengagement in public affairs and politics by American youth and young adults. As the evidence of a strong generational factor in civic disengagement accumulates, more attention is being given as well to how educational activities might foster youth appreciation of the value of participating in public life and for acquiring the knowledge and skills to do so. The collection is cosponsored by the Task Force on Civic Education of the American Political Science Association (APSA) and is one result of the initiatives of many Task Force members and their outreach on behalf of civic education. The Task Force was established at the initiative of Elinor Ostrom when she was President of the APSA in 1997. The Task Force "Articulation Statement" specifies its objectives. See Appendix B (list of Task Force members and Appendix C ("Articulation Statement").

*Education for Civic Engagement in Democracy: Service Learning and Other Promising Practices* brings together evidence of youth disengagement and reports on promising practices for civic education. The authors are scholars and educators from several academic disciplines: political science, communications, education, and public administration. They present different theoretical perspectives and instructional strategies. But, they all acknowledge the importance of making civic and political questions meaningful to students and doing so with instructional strategies that involve students directly in civic and political activities.

Several chapters in the collection are devoted to research findings on the impact of service and service learning and to programs that connect service to politics and public life more broadly. Volunteering in community service programs is meaningful to younger Americans.

Community service is being encouraged and increasingly required in some states and a growing number of schools on the reasoning that service will encourage not only students' appreciation for diversity and for assisting other people, but also a sense of civic duty. But, volunteering and even mandating community service does not automatically foster student participation in public life and democratic processes. Researchers, faculty, teachers, and community service directors will find the coverage devoted to service and service learning useful to their inquiries and applications of service learning.

The other practices explored in this collection are designed specifically to counter student cynicism and lack of information or misinformation about political processes and public officials. These practices prepare students to seek information about politics and government, participate in public affairs, and consider careers in public service.

The preparation of *Education for Civic Engagement in Democracy: Service Learning and Other Promising Practices* is due, in large part, to the commitment of the contributing authors to sharing their research with a wider audience of social scientists, educators, curriculum supervisors, and the concerned public. Its publication is the result of a collaboration among the ERIC Clearinghouse for Social Studies/Social Science Education, the American Political Science Association, and the Adjunct ERIC Clearinghouse for Service Learning.

Sheilah Mann
June 26, 2000

# 1

## Introduction to Education for Civic Engagement in Democracy

*John J. Patrick*

During the last ten years civic leaders and scholars have expressed great concern about civic and political apathy in the United States, especially among young Americans. A report of the National Commission on Civic Renewal, for example, warns, "In a time that cries out for civic action, we are in danger of becoming a nation of spectators" (1998, 6). Several commentators concur that the comprehensive civic condition of the United States is weaker than it was, and it needs to be improved. There has been a steady decrease in the engagement of citizens in their civil society and government, which is both an indicator and consequence of declining health in political and civic life (American Civic Forum 1994; Eisenhower Leadership Group 1996; Lipset 1995; Putnam 1995).

Robert D. Putnam's new book, *Bowling Alone: The Collapse and Revival of American Community* (2000), is the latest and strongest case about the decline of civic engagement and political participation in the United States, the need for civic renewal, and the means to achieve it. Putnam concludes, "Americans are playing virtually every aspect of the civic game less frequently today than we did two decades ago" (2000, 41).

Putnam duly recognizes the increasing numbers of regional and national "mass-membership organizations" like AARP (American Association of Retired Persons) and the AAA (American Automobile Association). He also notes the limited or nonexistent connectedness of most members whose "only act of membership consists in writing a check for dues or perhaps occasionally reading a newsletter" (2000, 52). Thus the unparalleled vitality of "mass-membership organizations" is not a reliable indicator of civic engagement in American society. Putnam concludes, "Many Americans continue to claim that we are members of various organizations, but most Americans no longer spend much time in community organizations – we've stopped doing committee work, stopped serving as officers, stopped going to meetings. . . . In short, Americans have been dropping out in droves, not merely from political life, but from organized community life more generally" (Putnam 2000, 63-64).

In Chapter 2 of this volume, Stephen Earl Bennett documents and discusses the prevailing political apathy and civic disengagement of American youth. Like Putnam, he identifies too many young Americans unwilling or incapable of assuming the responsibilities of democratic citizenship. And like Putnam, Bennett fears that if this trend is not reversed, democracy in the United States will be at risk.

The well-documented decline of civic engagement and political participation certainly is a threat to the quality of democracy in the United States. From antiquity to modernity, political theorists and practitioners have stressed the fundamental importance of civic engagement and political participation to the vitality of democracy. They also have emphasized the importance of effective civic education for the development of citizens with capacities to sustain a healthy democracy. Putnam agrees; he recommends a revitalized and improved civic education at the core of the school curriculum – "not just 'how a bill becomes a law,' but how can I participate effectively in the public life of my community?" (Putnam 2000, 405). This kind of reconstructed civic education could contribute mightily to a revival of civic and political engagement contend Putnam and others.

Is it possible for civic education in schools to be an effective agent of civic development among American youth? The results of the 1998 National Assessment of Educational Progress (NAEP) certainly temper our enthusiasm about the potential of schools to develop civic competence among most students. According to NAEP, three levels of achievement – *basic, proficient,* and *advanced* – specify the expectations of student performance in civics at grades four, eight, and twelve. The *basic* level represents partial mastery of knowledge and intellectual skills that are prerequisites to competence in civics. The *proficient* level designates fully competent performance. The *advanced* level signifies superior achievement in civics. In the 1998 NAEP in civics, the basic level of achievement was attained by 46% of students at grade four, 48% at grade eight, and 39% at grade twelve. The proficient level was reached by 21% of students at grade four, 21% at grade eight, and 22% at grade twelve. The advanced level was achieved by 2% of students at grade four, 2% at grade eight, and 4% at grade twelve. Another way to look at the overall findings is to note that 31% of the fourth-grade students were below the basic level of achievement and 69% were above it; at grade eight, 29% were below and 71% were above the basic level; and at grade twelve, 35% were below and 65% were above the basic level (Lutkus et al. 1999).

These disappointing NAEP results do not necessarily mean that civic education in schools cannot have a positive impact on students. On the contrary, systematic reviews of research in civic education suggest the potential effectiveness of particular curricular designs and methods of instruction (Nie, Junn & Stehlik-Berry 1996; Niemi & Junn 1998). The most promising practices involve systematic teaching and learning of key ideas about the substance of democracy throughout the elementary and secondary school curriculum. As students mature, they should encounter and use the same interconnected core concepts in cycles of increasing depth and complexity and in relationship to an ever-broader scope of information. Further, effective civic education includes application of core concepts to analysis and appraisal of public issues and problems of democracy. And it involves ample opportunities for learners to discuss ideas and otherwise interact with one another, as they confront issues and problems of democratic government and citizenship. So systematic exposure to key ideas and systematic practice in applying them to the organization and interpretation of information, issues, and problems is "what makes students learn" the requisites of constructive and enlightened civic engagement (Niemi & Junn 1998, 117-146).

Effective civic education conjoins teaching and learning of core content and cognitive processes – basic subject matter and skills of thinking that all students should be expected to achieve. To elevate one over the other – core content over cognitive processes or vice versa – is a pedagogical flaw that impedes achievement of knowledge. Further, some ideas, information, and issues should be viewed by teachers and learners as more important and thereby more worthy of emphasis in the school curriculum than other subject matter. Students should be taught that all knowledge is not equal in its value for constructive engagement in political and civic life. For example, concepts and principles on the substance of democracy are prerequisites to the development and maintenance of an active and responsible community of self-governing citizens. Without this kind of common civic knowledge, which should be developed through common learning experience in school, citizens are unable to act together to analyze public policy issues or problems, make cogent decisions about them, or participate intelligently to resolve them.

Civic knowledge and intellectual or cognitive skills certainly are necessary components of effective civic education. But there is more to it; participatory skills and civic dispositions in combination with essential civic knowledge and cognitive skills constitute a comprehensive conceptualization of civic education. See Figure 1.1 on page 5 (Patrick 1999, 34).

Basic knowledge must be applied effectively and responsibly to civic life if it would serve the needs of citizens and their *civitas*. Thus, a central facet of civic education should be the joint development of cognitive and participatory skills. Cognitive skills empower citizens to identify, describe, explain, and evaluate information and ideas pertinent to public issues and problems and to make and defend decisions about them. Participatory skills empower citizens to influence public policy decisions and to hold accountable their representatives in government. In combination cognitive and participatory skills are tools of citizenship in democracy whereby individuals, whether acting alone or in groups, can participate effectively to promote personal and common interests, to secure their rights, and to promote the common good.

The development of cognitive and participatory skills requires active learning by students inside and outside the classroom. Students should continually be challenged to use information and ideas, individually and collectively, to analyze case studies, respond to public issues, and resolve or meliorate political or civic problems.

A final component of education for citizenship in democracy pertains to virtues and dispositions, the traits of character necessary to the preservation and improvement of democracy. If citizens would enjoy the privileges and rights of their *civitas*, they must take responsibility for them, which requires a certain measure of civic virtue, such as self-discipline, civility, honesty, trust, courage, compassion, tolerance, and respect for the worth and dignity of all individuals. These characteristics can be nurtured through various social agencies in concert with schools.

A well-designed and well-taught curriculum on democratic citizenship includes the four components of Figure 1.1. This kind of civic education can yield citizens with deep understanding of the essential concepts and principles of democracy, strong commitment to them based on reason, high capacity for using them to analyze, appraise, and decide about the issues and problems of the political world, and competence to act effectively as engaged citizens in democracy to influence civil society and government.

---

### Figure 1.1

### Components of Education for Citizenship in Democracy

1. **Knowledge of Citizenship and Government in Democracy**
   a. Concepts and principles on the substance of democracy
   b. Ongoing tensions in civil society and government that raise public issues
   c. Constitutions and institutions of democratic government
   d. Functions of democratic institutions
   e. Practices of democratic citizenship and the roles of citizens
   f. Contexts of democracy: cultural, social, political, and economic
   g. History of democracy in particular states and throughout the world

2. **Cognitive Skills of Citizenship in Democracy**
   a. Identifying and describing phenomena or events of political and civic life
   b. Analyzing and explaining phenomena or events of political and civic life
   c. Evaluating, taking, and defending positions on public events and issues
   d. Making decisions on public issues
   e. Thinking critically about conditions of political and civic life
   f. Thinking constructively about how to improve political and civic life

3. **Participatory Skills of Citizenship in Democracy**
   a. Interacting with other citizens to promote personal and common interests
   b. Monitoring public events and issues
   c. Deliberating about public policy issues
   d. Influencing policy decisions on public issues
   e. Implementing policy decisions on public issues

4. **Dispositions of Citizenship in Democracy**
   a. Promoting the general welfare or common good of the community
   b. Recognizing the common humanity and dignity of each person
   c. Respecting, protecting, and exercising rights possessed equally by each person
   d. Participating responsibly and effectively in political and civic life
   e. Taking responsibility for government by consent of the governed
   f. Becoming a self-governing person by practicing civic virtues
   g. Supporting and maintaining democratic principles and practices

---

The authors of this volume, in chapters 3-12, discuss promising practices of citizenship education, which fit, more or less, the four components of Figure 1. None of these practices of education for civic engagement in democracy pertains exactly to every facet of the four components in Figure 1.1. All of them, however, are compatible with various parts of the conceptualization of civic education presented in Figure 1.1. Further, the authors of chapters 3-12 stress the importance of connections and interactions of knowledge, skills, and dispositions. Finally, they urge relationships between classroom lessons and the realities of civic and political life in the community outside the school.

Like Robert Putnam in *Bowling Alone: The Collapse and Revival of American Community*, the authors of chapters 3-12 agree that effective civic education in schools and other social agencies is a key to the renewal of civic engagement in American democracy. Like Putnam, they recommend rejection of the stale and dry traditional civics and advocate fresh content and pedagogy that involve students actively and collaboratively in lessons about real public issues and problems involving rights and responsibilities of citizenship in their own communities.

In Chapters 3 and 4, Richard M. Battistoni and Mary A. Hepburn make the case for well-designed service learning as one promising means to education for civic engagement in democracy. They discuss research-based practices in service learning likely to be effective in development of student civic competencies. In particular, Battistoni and Hepburn emphasize the worth of service-learning programs that connect systematically elements of all four components of civic education in Figure 1.1.

In Chapter 5, Harry C. Boyte reports on the Public Achievement project of the Center for Democracy and Citizenship in Minnesota, which is based on his "public work" method of civic education through service-learning activities. Boyte emphasizes cooperation among students involved in community-based activities for the public good. Participants develop civic skills and dispositions that enable them to become continual contributors to their commonwealth.

In Chapter 6, Iara Peng discusses the content and methods of teaching and learning of the National Issues Forums (NIF). She emphasizes development of civic knowledge and cognitive skills through the practice of deliberation and decision making about hot public issues.

The acclaimed *Kids Voting USA* curriculum is the subject of Chapter 7 by Steven Chaffee. He discusses lessons of a curriculum that interrelate civic knowledge, cognitive skills, participatory skills, and civic dispositions about elections and voter behavior. He also reports findings of research about the positive effects of the *Kids Voting USA* curriculum on students and their parents.

Herbert M. Atherton of the Center for Civic Education in Calabasas, California treats CCE's *Project Citizen*, which involves students in analysis and choice about the alternatives of community-based issues. *Project Citizen* is used throughout the United States. Further, it has been implemented in the curriculum of schools in many countries in various regions of the world. *Project Citizen* is designed to develop cognitive skills, participatory skills, and dispositions of citizenship in democracy through activities that involve cooperative learning by students in small groups.

Civic education programs of the Dirksen Congressional Center in Pekin, Illinois are reported by Frank H. Mackaman and Andrea Schade in Chapter 9. These creative programs emphasize teaching and learning about the United States Congress in ways that motivate students and involve them in active learning of knowledge and cognitive skills.

In Chapter 10, John G. Stone III presents the concept of the public service academy, which involves "a school-within-a-school" that stresses education about public service through government. Thus, students develop civic knowledge and skills of democratic citizenship. Further, they may be motivated to pursue public service careers in government or other organizations that serve the people in democracy.

In Chapter 11, Susan A. MacManus discusses cynicism and apathy and other factors that disable students from pursuing careers in politics and government. She also discusses what civic educators can do to counteract negative perceptions about public service and political life and to teach students accurately and compellingly about civics and government.

Finally, in Chapter 12 Jan Goehring, Karl Kurtz, and Alan Rosenthal treat methods of teaching and learning that promote civic engagement and warranted trust in government. The authors highlight their "new public perspective on representative democracy" that can counter the current widespread negative perceptions of politics and government in American democracy.

Chapters 2-12 collectively respond to current trends of civic disengagement and propose practices of civic education that have potential to stimulate revival of civic and political life in the United States. Thus, they react positively to the challenge posed in *Bowling Alone: The Collapse and Revival of American Community*. "Let us find ways to ensure that by 2010 many more Americans will participate in the public life of our communities – running for office, attending public meetings, serving on committees, campaigning in elections, and even voting" (Putnam 2000, 412). Reforms of civic education in schools, such as those suggested by the authors of Chapters 2-12, appear to be necessary if not sufficient means to address Putnam's challenge. In concert with other efforts in various agencies of our American society, these recommended practices of civic education have the potential to make a positive difference in the civic and political life of democracy in the United States of America.

## References

American Civic Forum. 1994. *Civic Declaration: A Call for a New Citizenship*. Dayton, OH: The Kettering Foundation.

Eisenhower Leadership Group. 1996. *Democracy at Risk: How Schools Can Lead*. College Park: Center for Political Leadership and Participation of the University of Maryland.

Lipset, Seymour Martin. 1995. "Malaise and Resiliency in America." *Journal of Democracy* 6 (July): 4-18.

Lutkus, Anthony et al. 1999. *NAEP 1998 Civics Report Card for the Nation*. Washington, DC: U.S. Department of Education.

National Commission on Civic Renewal. 1998. *A Nation of Spectators: How Civic Disengagement Weakens America and What We Can Do About It*. College Park: Institute for Philosophy and Public Policy, University of Maryland.

Nie, Norman H., Jane Junn, and Kenneth Stehlik-Barry. 1996. *Education and Democratic Citizenship in America*. Chicago: The University of Chicago Press.

Niemi, Richard G., and Jane Junn. 1998. *Civic Education: What Makes Students Learn*. New Haven, CT: Yale University Press.

Patrick, John J. 1999. "Concepts at the Core of Education for Democratic Citizenship." In *Principles and Practices of Education for Democratic Citizenship: International Perspective and Projects*, Charles F. Bahmueller and John J. Patrick, eds. Bloomington, IN: ERIC Clearinghouse for Social Studies/Social Science Education.

Putnam, Robert D. 1995. "Tuning In, Tuning Out: The Strange Disappearance of Social Capital in America." PS: *Political Science and Politics* 28 (December): 664-683.

Putnam, Robert D. 2000. *Bowling Alone: The Collapse and Revival of American Community*. New York: Simon & Schuster.

# 2

# Political Apathy and Avoidance of News Media Among Generations X and Y: America's Continuing Problem

*Stephen Earl Bennett*

This is a study of political apathy and avoidance of traditional political news among young people in the United States of America. Data from recent polls show young people are profoundly disconnected from public affairs. If large slices of Generations X and Y are politically indifferent and avoid the news media, democracy's future dims considerably (People for the American Way 1989, 11; Dahl 1998, 37-38). The United States faces a quandary about its youth, many of whom cannot fulfill their obligations as democratic citizens. Some means must be found to overcome youthful indifference to politics; otherwise, the future of America's democratic experiment looks bleak.

Five studies illustrate the problem we face among young people today, and provide the backdrop against which the chapter is written. First, according to the 1998 National Assessment of Educational Progress in civics, most high school seniors lack sufficient understanding of government to act intelligently as voters (Lutkus et al. 1999). Second, the American Council of Trustees and Alumni's recent poll finds that seniors at the nation's top 55 institutions of higher education are woefully ignorant of United States history (Morin 2000).[1] Third, the Gallup poll of American teens, taken between January and April of 2000, finds widespread ignorance of key facts about American history (Gallup & Gallup 2000). Fourth, UCLA's Higher Education Research Institute's survey of first-year college students in 1999 shows a continuing pattern of political disengagement among the nation's youth, one the Institute had identified earlier (Sax et

9

al. 1998, 1999; also see Mann 1999 for a political scientist's assessment of the Institute's 1998 data). Fifth, the John F. Kennedy School of Government's Shorenstein Center, as part of its "Vanishing Voter Project," finds "pervasive apathy" among young adults ("Vanishing Voter" 2000). According to the Center, "political apathy characterizes young people in nearly every demographic category."

Young people's political inattentiveness and ignorance stem from inadequate civics instruction (Janowitz 1983) and indifference to government and public affairs (Bennett 1986; Delli Carpini & Keeter 1996; Niemi & Junn 1998). High school seniors continue a pattern of political indifference typical of recent entrants into the American electorate (Bennett 1997, 1998; Mann 1999).

### Birth Cohorts and American Democracy

A new birth cohort is emerging on the political scene, consisting of persons born after 1978.[2] Although they have been labeled the "Ambitious Generation" (Schneider and Stevenson 1999) or "Echo Boomers" (*American Demographics* 1999), calling them Generation Y links them to Generation X. Generation Y joins Generation X (Americans born between 1965 and 1978) as the youngest members of the American electorate. As such, Generation Y's and Generation X's political apathy and media habits may be harbingers of what the United States can expect as each year adds another segment of Gen-Yers to the voting-age population. (This assumes that younger segments of Generation Y are like those who are already of voting age, which evidently they are [see National Association of Secretaries of State 1999].) As we shall see, Gen-Yers and Gen-Xers are not all that different when it comes to apathy and avoidance of the traditional news media.

The two birth cohorts' indifference to politics and tendency to eschew exposure to traditional print and electronic news media are worrisome. Psychological involvement in public affairs and media habits are indicators of engagement in the nation's political life. In order to put today's youth into proper relief, I shall compare current patterns of those of similar-aged individuals from previous decades, which is always a risky enterprise. Fortunately, we have good evidence on youths' political attitudes and behavior in the 1950s, 1960s, and 1970s.[3]

Most of the data comes from polls conducted for the Pew Research Center for The People & The Press, one in April and May of 1998, another in June of that year, the November 1998 "Technology" poll, and the August 1999 "Values" poll (Pew Center 1998a, 1998b, 1999a, 1999b).[4] At the time the polls were conducted, members of Generation Y were 18 to 20 years old. I will also use a Gallup Poll done for the *Times Mirror* Center for The People & The Press in May, 1987 (*Times Mirror* 1987).[5] The 1998, 1999, and 1987 polls permit comparisons of Gen-Yers with Gen-Xers born between 1968 and 1970 – when they were similarly aged.

Anemic citizenship among the youngest members of the public might not be alarming if the rest of the populace manifested vigorous civic engagement. Once upon a time, youthful apathy gave way to political engagement as individuals progressed through the life cycle (Converse with Niemi 1971). Unhappily, many Americans disconnect from society today. Whether the topic be waning social capital (Putnam 1995a, 1995b; Rahn 1998; Rahn & Transue 1998) or civic disengagement (National Commission on Civic Renewal 1998), there are grounds for concern about America's future.

## Two Caveats about Assessing the Young

Two caveats must be made at the outset of any discussion of young people. First, adults' tendency to identify wayward attitudes and conduct among the young is well-established. Writers found fault with American youth in the 1920s and 1930s (see, for example, Allen 1961, 1964). Today, those same "errant" young are "the greatest generation" (Brokaw 1998). Whatever history writes about the Baby Boomers, one recalls mixed observations about them when they were young (*cf.* Altbach 1974; Flacks 1971, with Feuer 1969), and even not so young (*cf.* Collier & Horowitz 1989; Delli Carpini 1986, with Light 1988; MacPherson 1984). Hence, in discussing today's young, we need to remember that a definitive judgment about them is a long way off.

Second, the more one observes today's youth, the more one gets a mixed impression. In many ways, young Americans are highly praiseworthy. A recent article in *US News & World Report*, for example, identified several positive trends among American teenagers: declining arrests for violent crimes, decreased use of alcohol and drugs, lower pregnancy rates, fewer school dropouts, and increased volunteering for community projects (Cannon & Kleiner 2000).

In other ways, however, young people are worrisome. I do not refer just to the assertion – now over a decade old – that many young persons postpone adopting adult roles (Littwin 1986). Not only are many teens and twenty-somethings driven by consumeristic fads (*American Demographics* 1999), cheating seems rampant at all education levels (Kleiner & Lord 1999). Many young people's cavalier attitude about academic honesty is particularly jarring, for it is difficult to jibe with the notion of civic virtue. Even those who find today's youth more ambitious than those of a generation or more ago confess that contemporary adolescents lack a sense of direction (Schneider & Stevenson 1999).

## Should We Care If Young People Are Apathetic?

Here the focus is on diverse facets of psychological involvement in public affairs. To put it baldly, young Americans eschew interest in, exposure to news of, and participation in the political process. Youthful indifference to politics is not new (Converse with Niemi 1971), of course, and low rates of voting by young Americans can probably be traced back to the twentieth century's early decades (Kleppner 1982). In her compendium on *Political Participation in the United States*, Margaret Conway summarizes a sizable corpus: "Young citizens are less likely to participate politically than are middle-aged citizens" (2000, 22).

Why be concerned about a phenomenon that has occurred for a long time? One could argue that non-voting by young people ought to occasion neither surprise nor concern, for turnout increases as people progress through the life cycle (Campbell, et al. 1960; Glenn & Grimes 1968; Jennings 1979; Wolfinger & Rosenstone 1980). Hence, if young people are not voting today, they will once they have finished schooling, taken a job, found a significant other, and settled into a community.

Although direct comparisons from one era to another are difficult, it appears that political disinterest and disengagement are more widespread and deeper than was true of young people in previous decades (*Times Mirror* 1990). As the *Times Mirror* Center noted (1990, 1), "today's young Americans, aged 18 to 30, know less and care less about news and public affairs than any other generation of Americans in the past 50 years." Sadly, youthful apathy, ignorance, and non-participation are even more pronounced today than when the *Times Mirror* Center made its observation.

## A First Look at Apathy Among the Young

The evidence for young people's political apathy appears in many guises, and can be found in many places. It goes further than abstention from voting, which is itself a very important behavior in modern democracy (Pomper 1988). Certainly if one believes that voting is democracy's most fundamental act, a high rate of abstention among the young is disturbing.

Moreover, abstention from the polls is more pronounced among the young today than as recently as the early 1970s. In 1972, for example, roughly 50 percent of 18-24 year-olds cast ballots in the first presidential election following ratification of the 26th Amendment to the U.S. Constitution. According to the Committee for the Study of the American Electorate, turnout among 18-24 year-olds was under 30 percent in 1996 and less than 15 percent in 1998 ( Less than ten percent of 18-29 year olds went to the polls in contested presidential primaries held before March 7, 2000 (Thau and Eisinger 2000).

Another indicator of youthful inattention to politics is their lack of interest in government and public affairs. Psychological involvement in public affairs, indicated by political interest, is a very important indicator of civic engagement. Jan Van Deth defines political interest as *"the degree to which politics arouses a citizen's curiosity"* (1990, 278). Following Robert Lane (1965, 143-46), Van Deth argues that "interest is a measure of the degree of motivation for political participation" (1990, 277). Political interest predicts a host of dispositions and behaviors, such as knowledge about public affairs, political participation, and – most important for our purposes – exposure to political media. As Philip Converse noted (1972), attention to politics is an excellent indicator of a public's political skills.

Probably because they accept the proposition that "being interested is a clearly recognizable experience" (Lazarsfeld, Berelson & Gaudet 1968, 41), many scholars rely on a single item tapping psychological involvement in public affairs (for example, Rahn 1998; Van Deth 1990; Verba, Schlozman & Brady 1995). In its June 1998, November 1998 and August 1999 polls, the Pew Center asked the general political interest question developed by the Survey Research Center for the 1964 National Election Study, as amended in 1968 (Bennett 1986):

> Some people seem to follow what's going on in the government and public affairs most of the time, whether there's an election going on or not. Others aren't that interested. Would you say you follow what's going on in government and public affairs most of the time, some of the time, only now and then, or hardly at all?

## Table 2.1

### General Political Interest by Birth Cohorts, 1999

| How Often R Follows Public Affairs | Older Birth Cohorts | Cold Warriors | Early Baby Boomers | Late Baby Boomers | Generation X | Generation Y |
|---|---|---|---|---|---|---|
| Most of the Time | 56% | 60% | 49% | 38% | 32% | 8% |
| Some of the Time | 23 | 23 | 33 | 40 | 32 | 41 |
| Only Now and Then | 17 | 12 | 14 | 14 | 26 | 37 |
| Hardly At All | 5 | 6 | 3 | 8 | 10 | 14 |
| Total | 100% | 100% | 100% | 100% | 100% | 100% |
| (N=) | (102) | (185) | (149) | (225) | (259) | (51) |

Source: The Pew Center's August 1999 "Values" poll.

Table 2.1 depicts Americans' general interest in politics in 1999, broken down by six birth cohorts: (1) persons born before 1930; (2) "Cold Warriors," or those born between 1930 and 1945; (3) Early Baby Boomers, who were born between 1946 and 1954; (4) Late Baby Boomers, who were born between 1955 and 1964; (5) Generation X, or those born between 1965 and 1978; and (6) members of Generation Y who were born in 1979 and 1980.[6]

The first impression one gains is that older birth cohorts are considerably more interested in politics than are younger Americans. The gap in political interest between the two oldest birth cohorts – those born before 1945 (and the two youngest cohorts) those born after 1965 – is substantial. Nearly three-fifths of the oldest cohorts say they follow public affairs most of the time, compared to roughly a third of Generation X and less than a tenth of Generation Y. (The 1998 poll shows approximately the same results.) Gen-Xers are the most apathetic segment of today's electorate.[7]

Although Baby Boomers fall midway between the two oldest and the two youngest cohorts, older Boomers are more politically attentive than younger Boomers. This finding reaffirms the importance of breaking the Baby Boom cohort into two segments, as earlier researchers have suggested (Bennett & Bennett 1990; Jennings & Niemi 1981). When they compared the high school senior class of 1965 (most of whom were born in

1947) with the class of 1973 (mostly born in 1955), Kent Jennings and Richard Niemi were struck by differences between the two cohorts (1981, 220-27). They concluded that "the 1973 cohort [w]as distinctly less imbued with the traditional virtues associated with civic training. Politics was less central in their lives and the participant culture less valued" (Jennings & Niemi 1981, 225).

## Comparing Generation Y with Generation X in 1987

Is this a generational or an aging phenomenon? One means to answer the question is to look at interest in 1987, when Gen-Xers who were born between 1968 and 1970 were 18 to 20 years old. The *Times Mirror*'s May, 1987 poll asked the same question as is depicted in Table 2.1. When the 1987 data are broken down by the same birth cohorts as in Table 2.1 – with the exception of breaking Generation X into those born between 1965 and 1967 and persons born in 1968 and 1970 – a mixed result occurs. The 18 and 20 year-olds in 1987 were more politically interested than Gen-Yers in 1999. A quarter of the 18-20 year-olds said they followed public affairs most of the time, while 37 percent said some of the time, 21 percent said only now and then, and 17 percent said hardly at all. Slightly older Gen-Xers were only a bit different from the 18 and 19 year-olds in 1987; the biggest difference was that only 11 percent of "twenty-something" Gen-Xers said they paid hardly any attention to all the public affairs, while 46 percent reported following public affairs some of the time.

Just as Table 2.1 shows, the two Baby Boom birth cohorts were slightly more interested than the Gen-Xers in 1987, but less so than the Cold Warriors and the oldest birth cohort. As usual, younger Baby Boomers were less politically attentive than older Boomers.

Although one cannot readily separate aging, cohort, and period effects with cross-sectional polls (Glenn 1977), the *Times Mirror*'s 1987 data and the Pew Center's 1998 and 1999 polls support claims that Gen-Xers and Gen-Yers tend to be indifferent to public affairs. (Although it is difficult to compare political interest when using *Times Mirror*/Pew Center data and National Election Studies, the 1972 NES shows that Early Baby Boomers who were 18-20 years old were roughly as apathetic as the same-aged Gen-Xers in 1987, but more politically interested than Gen-Yers were in 1998 and 1999; eighteen-to-20-year-olds in 1972 were born in 1952 and 1954.)

One way to get better purchase on Generation Y's apathy is to look at the impact of its educational attainment on political interest. Education's importance for psychological involvement in public affairs is well-known (Almond & Verba 1963; Verba, Schlozman & Brady 1995). Moreover, education is usually the strongest demographic predictor of political interest (Converse 1972, 1974).

**Table 2.2**

**Birth Cohorts' Interest in Politics, by Education in 1987 and 1998[a]**

|  | Older Birth Cohorts | Cold Warriors | Early Baby Boomers | Late Baby Boomers | Generation X | 18 & 19 Year Olds |
|---|---|---|---|---|---|---|
| 1987 | | | | | | |
| LT High School Grad | 35 | 26 | 17 | 20 | 15 | 26 |
| High School Grad | 52 | 42 | 30 | 29 | 15 | 16 |
| Some College | 70 | 56 | 52 | 34 | 37 | 41 |
| College Grad | 78 | 67 | 64 | 49 | 40 | — |
| 1998 | | | | | | |
| LT High School Grad | 34 | 35 | 31 | 34 | 21 | 35 |
| High School Grad | 54 | 50 | 38 | 34 | 24 | 11 |
| Some College | 65 | 65 | 47 | 44 | 29 | 29 |
| College Grad | 72 | 73 | 63 | 55 | 39 | — |

[a]Entries are the percentage of each education category that reported following public affairs most of the time.

Sources: May 1987 Gallup poll for the *Times Mirror* Center and merged data from the Pew Research Center's June 1998 and November 1998 polls.

Table 2.2 shows birth cohorts' political interest by level of formal schooling in 1987 and 1998. (The Pew Center's August 1999 poll has too few cases to provide meaningful analyses when a variable such as education is controlled. The 1987 data are now based only on 18 and 19 year-olds, to be consistent with the merged 1998 polls.) These data clearly show the combined effects of aging and education on political interest. In both years, as people's level of formal schooling went up, they tended to be more attentive to politics. Moreover, with the possible exception of those with less than complete high school, the older birth cohorts are more politically interested than their younger, similarly schooled, compatriots.

Note also how eleven years' passage affects interest among the least educated of the two Boomer cohorts. Only a fifth of Late Baby Boomers whose education stopped before completing high school said they followed politics most of the time in 1987; by 1998, a third of them did. One sees even more gain in interest among the least educated Early Baby Boomer cohort, the percentage of this group that said they were more attentive to politics nearly doubled.

For our purposes, however, the most important pattern occurs among the 18 and 19 year-olds in both years. This is the only segment of the populace that does not manifest a monotonic relationship between education and interest in politics. Interestingly, in both years, 18 and 19 year-olds whose formal schooling ended before the twelfth grade reported greater interest than the high school graduates. No other education/cohort category was as politically indifferent as Gen-Yers who were high school graduates in 1998. At that, teen-aged high school graduates in 1987 were only slightly less apathetic. Since high school graduates made up 51 percent of the Gen-Yers in 1998, and 46 percent of the youngest Generation X high school graduates in 1987, we have a good handle on why the two youngest groupings were the most apathetic segment of the 1987 and 1998 electorates.

Another tidbit raises an interesting puzzle. The 18 and 19 year-olds in both years are disproportionately male (slightly over three-fifths). Young men are also more likely than young women to drop out of high school; twenty percent of Generation Y women were high school drop-outs in 1998, versus 30 percent of male Gen-Yers. Moreover, lesser educated young men are less attentive to politics than comparably schooled young women.

That is a new trend, and it needs to be better understood. As recently as a decade ago, American women tended to be less interested in politics than men, regardless of age and educational attainment (Bennett & Bennett 1989).

Although scholars need to discover why apathy is more prevalent among poorly educated young men than among similarly educated young women, there is little mystery about political indifference among young people in general. Morris Janowitz (1983) detailed declining efforts to inculcate civic values in the public schools, beginning immediately after World War II. Recent efforts to include experiential education via community service in curricula are tacit admission of the schools' futility using traditional pedagogy (Battistoni & Hudson 1997; Ehrlich 1998). Although scholars once believed that civics courses were of little use (Langton & Jennings 1968), recent research suggests otherwise (Niemi and Junn 1998). The data in Tables 2.1 and 2.2 add to concern about how well America's schools inculcate a civic ethic in today's youth.

### Youthful Avoidance of the News Media

Political indifference among Generation Y would be of limited importance if it had little impact on behavior. Unfortunately, apathy has palpable consequences, especially when it comes to exposure to political media.

### Table 2.3

### Exposure to the Mass Media by Birth Cohorts, 1998

| Read/Watch Listen | Older Birth Cohorts | Cold Warriors | Early Baby Boomers | Late Baby Boomers | Generation X | Generation Y |
|---|---|---|---|---|---|---|
| Newspaper[a] | 83 | 77 | 75 | 66 | 61 | 61 |
| Network TV News[a] | 59 | 54 | 43 | 33 | 25 | 19 |
| Local TV News[a] | 77 | 72 | 65 | 65 | 55 | 49 |
| News on Radio[a] | 46 | 49 | 64 | 58 | 50 | 44 |
| MTV[a] | 4 | 3 | 2 | 3 | 9 | 36 |
| Access Internet/ WWW[b] | 9 | 25 | 45 | 48 | 54 | 58 |

[a]"Regularly" Read/Watch/Listen
[b]"Ever" Go Online to Access the Internet or the World Wide Web
Source: For Newspapers through MTV, the Pew Center's May 1998 poll. For Internet/ WWW, the Pew Center's November 1998 "Technology" poll

Table 2.3 depicts exposure to print and electronic news media by the same birth cohorts that Table 2.1 depicts. The dependent variables include each cohort's exposure to newspapers, local TV newscasts, the nightly network news shows, radio news broadcasts, MTV, and the Internet or World Wide Web. With the exception of the item about the Internet/WWW, the entries are the percentage of each birth cohort that reported regularly relying on the media. Most of the data come from the Pew Center's May 1998 poll. The last question appeared on the Center's November 1998 Technology poll and asked if respondents ever go on-line to access the Internet or the World Wide Web. The Center's August 1999 poll also asked several questions about exposure to print and electronic news media, and going on the Internet and/or WWW.

Looking at newspapers, Gen-Yers are as likely to say they are regular readers as are Gen-Xers, although these cohorts are less likely regularly to read a paper than are Early Baby Boomers, Cold Warriors, and the Older Birth Cohorts. When the Pew Center's August 1999 poll asked if people had read a paper the day before being interviewed, 31 percent of Generation Y said yes, as did 35 percent of Generation X, 47 percent of the Late Baby Boomers, 50 percent of the Early Boomers, 57 percent of the Cold Warriors, and 73 percent of the oldest birth cohorts.

The Center's 1998 polls show that Gen-Yers are 34 percentage points less likely to report reading a paper "yesterday" than to say they regularly read a newspaper. No other birth cohort manifests so large a decline in reading when the question shifts from regular newspaper reading to reading the paper the day before being interviewed.

When it comes to local and national television newscasts, members of Generation Y are less likely than other birth cohorts to be regular members of the audience. The pattern is especially true for network newscasts. The cohort gap in watching the network newscasts grows even larger when people are asked if they watched a network TV newscast the day before being interviewed. Fifty-one percent of Gen-Yers said they watched the news on television "yesterday," which is 31 percentage points less than the oldest cohort, and 21 points below the Cold Warriors.

Although there are some cohort-related differences, members of Generation Y are just as likely to report hearing political news on radio as the two oldest cohorts, which may reflect age-related patterns of listening to radio in general. On the other hand, Gen-Yers are most likely to be regular members of MTV's audience. They are several times more likely to watch MTV than are Early and Late Boomers, Cold Warriors, and the Older Birth Cohorts. Generations Y and X are also more likely to have accessed the Internet or the World Wide Web. The August 1999 poll shows that, although three-fifths of Baby Boomers report going on-line to access the Internet or WWW, or to send and receive e-mail, three quarters of Gen-Xers and Gen-Yers report doing so. (By contrast only four percent of the older birth cohorts, and only 36 percent of the Cold Warriors say they have gone on-line.)

When asked why they are unlikely to read newspapers and watch TV newscasts, young people frequently claim they are too busy. The data on exposure to MTV and accessing the Internet or World Wide Web, however, belie the claim (see also Pew Center 1996).

The Pew Center's May 1998 poll provides useful purchase on the reasons behind members of Generation Y's tendency to eschew political news. When respondents were asked how much they looked forward to getting the news, one-fifth of the 18 and 19 year-olds responded "a lot," compared with two-fifths of Gen-Xers and Late Boomers, and 56 to 69 percent of the older birth cohorts (Early Boomers, Cold Warriors, and the Older Birth Cohorts). Similarly, when the Pew Center asked respondents who said they regularly read a newspaper how much they would miss one if they could not get it, about two-fifths of Gen-Yers said "a lot," compared to over half of the Gen-Xers and Late Boomers, and 60-70 percent of the Late Boomers, Cold Warriors, and Older Birth Cohorts. Many Gen-Yers would not miss a newspaper and avoid electronic news media because they do not look forward to getting the news.

### Are There Any Reasons for Youthful Apathy Today?

Two facets of Generation Y shed light on this cohort's political passivity. Today's youthful indifference to politics is exacerbated by lack of identification with established political parties. The Pew Center's August 1999 poll shows that only 12 percent of Gen-Yers strongly identify with one of the major political parties, while 31 percent are weak partisans and 57 percent are Independents. Gen-Yers are less partisan than their "elders," including Gen-Xers. Converse and Niemi (1971) noted a tendency toward independence among young people in the 1950s, which they believed contributed to political indifference. A lack of partisan proclivities among today's young is far more prevalent than was true of young people in the 1950s (Flanigan & Zingale 1998, 80-82).

The August 1999 poll also shows that 29 percent of Gen-Yers claim to work full-time, while 50 percent are part-time workers. Early entry into the workforce is a hallmark of young people today (Schneider & Stevenson 1999, 170), out-stripping youthful employment as recently as the 1980s (Starr 1986). Although the number of cases is small, the data suggest that full-time employment among Gen-Yers resonates with political indifference.

The reasons for heavy work schedules among today's young are beyond our scope. Suffice it to say that political attentiveness may be another casualty of Generation Y's involvement in the workforce. Women's entry into the workforce in the 1970s, particularly if the job was uninspiring, did not guarantee greater political engagement (McDonagh 1982), and the same may hold for Gen-Yers today.

There are many causes for concern about today's young, from Curtis Gans' estimate that only 11 percent of the 18 and 19 year-olds voted in 1998 to evidence that they are indifferent to public affairs, eschew exposure to political media, pay little or no heed to news about local, national, and international events, and increasingly distrust other citizens (Rahn & Transue 1998). If nothing else gives pause, consider 1998's survey of college first-year students conducted by UCLA's Higher Education Research Institute, which shows they are profoundly disconnected from public affairs (Mann 1999; Sax et al. 1998). Linda Sax and her colleagues found, for example, that only 26 percent of college freshmen in 1998 thought that "keeping up to date with political affairs" is a very important or essential life goal, compared to 58 percent in 1966. Only 14 percent of freshmen in 1998 reported "frequently" discussing politics, compared with 30 percent in 1968 (Sax et al. 1998, 4).

Some, seeking evidence to counter assertions about youthful avoidance of public affairs, point to indications of rising levels of "volunteering" among the young. Although recent H.E.R.I. polls show growth in the percentage of first-year college students who say they have done volunteer work, the 1998 poll indicates these people do not place much value on the activity (Mann 1999; Sax et al. 1998). A growing number of secondary schools require "volunteer" work for graduation. Forcing young people to "volunteer" may be laudable, but forced "volunteering" is not the same as willingly engaging in an act. The 1999 "College Freshmen" poll found, for example, that although three-quarters of first-year students reported engaging in volunteer work as high school seniors, there were indications of declining commitment to social activism, environmentalism, and social consciousness (Sax et al. 1999, 5- 6).

Before closing, an obvious question is "aren't these patterns normal?" At first blush, they are. The young were less politically engaged than their elders in the 1950s and early 1960s (Converse with Niemi 1971). Today's patterns, however, are more pronounced than those of yesteryear (see also *Times Mirror* 1990). Even if we look at the 1987 poll, we see that 18-20 year-olds were less likely than their elders to report reading a paper or paying attention to local or national news on TV. The cohort-based gap, however, was considerably smaller than today's. Moreover, political socialization research in the 1950s and 1960s found young people were more politically interested and attentive than the data above indicate about today's youth (Hess & Torney 1967; Jennings & Niemi 1974, 1981).

If we value informed participation in the political arena, we should be concerned about Gen-Yers' political indifference and avoidance of political media. Generation Yers who are politically apathetic and eschew political media fail to meet the "effective participation" and "enlightened understanding" criteria that Robert Dahl says are essential for a democracy (1998). The Pew Center's data show, for example, that Gen-Yers who are apathetic, do not read a newspaper, or do not watch the news on TV, are less likely to be registered to vote than are those who are politically interested, read a paper regularly or the day before being interviewed, and watch TV newscasts regularly or "yesterday." Moreover, although the measure of public affairs knowledge is crude, the Pew Center's May 1998 poll shows that Gen-Yers who abstain from exposure to political media are less informed than those who regularly read a newspaper or watch television news shows.

## What Can Be Done?

Can anything be done to heighten Generation Y's civic engagement? (Some say it may already be too late for Generation X.) The American Political Science Association's attempts to rebuild civic education may achieve a laudable goal (APSA Task Force 1998). Some doubt the APSA's effort will bear fruit (Leonard 1999), while others are at least guardedly optimistic (Schachter 1998). A few scholar-teachers can point to successful programs (Ehrlich 1998). Efforts to have students follow and examine current events and news reports about public affairs, such as those by The New York Times, the Gannet and Knight-Ridder program, and the Center for Civic Education's multi-state programs may bear useful fruit.

As have other disciplines – mathematics, the natural sciences, and economics, for example – political scientists should work with parent-teachers' associations, the schools, and state legislators to insist that civics and government teachers are better trained. Advertisements plumping newspaper reading may have some benefits, particularly if the campaign is targeted at teenagers. TV networks must also find some means to appeal to a younger audience. Political parties have a stake in connecting young people – presumably without congealed partisan ties – to the process of government. Public officials, many of whom cater to older, well-off members of the electorate, need to be reminded that the future belongs to the young. (It is not surprising to learn that the Pew Center's August 1999 poll found 73 percent of Gen-Yers agree that "[i]t is time for Washington politicians to step aside and make room for new leaders," and 41 percent concurred that "[w]e need new people in Washington, even if they are not as effective as experienced leaders.")

## Conclusion

Unless we find some means to overcome young Americans' detachment from and dislike of politics, America's experiment with popular government will be at risk. Democracy calls for concern and effort by its citizenry, and the youngest birth cohorts in the electorate appear ill-prepared for those responsibilities. A decade ago, the People for the American Way (1989) called attention to the problem, and the recent report by the National Association of Secretaries of State (1999) shows that little has changed. We have work to do.

## Notes

1. When we deal with university students, it is well to recall we are dealing with America's "best and brightest." Hence, if these young people manifest political indifference and ignorance, we see just part of a larger problem.

2. Scholars agree that picking the beginning and ending years for any birth cohort is tricky (Mannheim 1952). The years used to date cohorts are taken from earlier research (Bennett and Bennett 1990; Rahn 1998). Strauss and Howe (1997), on the other hand, date what they call the "Millennial Generation" from 1982 onward.

3. The 1950s and 1960s were the "golden age" for political socialization research (see, for example, Easton and Dennis 1969; Greenstein 1969; Hess and Torney 1967; Jaros 1973; Jennings and Niemi 1974, 1981; Langton 1969; Niemi 1974; Sigel and Hoskin 1981; compendia by Conover 1991; Kinder and Sears 1985; and Sears 1975; and collections of original research edited by Adler and Harrington 1970; Bell 1973; Dennis 1973; Orum 1972; Schwartz and Schwartz 1975; Renshon 1977; and Sigel 1965, 1969. Unfortunately, studies of how young people acquire political attitudes and behaviors became rare after the political socialization field suffered seemingly devastating critiques, especially by Donald Searing and his associates (1973, 1976). Happily, there is evidence of a renewed interest in the field (see, for example, Niemi and Junn 1998).

4. The Pew Center succeeded the *Times Mirror* Center in January 1996. These polls were released directly by the Center. I wish to thank Dr. Andrew Kohut, Director of the Center, and the staff for their assistance. I am responsible for all analyses and interpretations.

5. Unlike the 1998 polls, which relied on telephone interviewing, the 1987 Gallup Poll was conducted in person. The sample had 4,244 cases.

6. Bennett and Bennett (1990, 110-115) develop the rationale behind these birth cohorts.

7. Since others have found that these are among the most residentially mobile segments of the public (Squire, Wolfinger, and Glass 1987), and mobility depresses political interest (Converse with Niemi 1971), we have an additional insight on apathy among the youngest members of the electorate.

## References

Adler, Norman, and Charles Harrington, eds. 1970. *The Learning of Political Behavior*. Glenview, IL: Scott Foresman.

Allen, Frederick Lewis. [1931] 1964. *Only Yesterday: An Informal History of the 1920s*. New York: Perennial Library.

Allen, Frederick Lewis [1940] 1961. *Since Yesterday*, 1929-1939. New York: Bantam.

Almond, Gabriel A., and Sidney Verba. 1963. *The Civic Culture: Political Attitudes and Democracy in Five Nations*. Princeton, NJ: Princeton University Press.

Altbach, Philip G. 1974. *Student Politics in America: A Historical Analysis*. New York: McGraw-Hill.

Alwin, Duane F. 1991. "Aging, Cohorts, and Social Change: An Examination of the Generational Replacement Model of Social Change." Presented at the VSB Masterclass "Dynamics of Cohort and Generations Research." University of Utrecht, The Netherlands.

American Demographics. 1999. "The Echo Boom Comes of Age." *American Demographics* 19 (September): <http://www.marketingtools.com/publications/ad990903d.htm>.

APSA Task Force on Civic Education for the Next Century. 1998. "Expanded Articulation Statement: A Call for Reactions and Contributions." *PS: Political Science and Politics* 31 (September): 636-637.

Battistoni, Richard M., and William E. Hudson, eds. 1997. *Experiencing Citizenship: Concepts and Models for Service-Learning in Political Science*. Washington, DC: American Association for High Education.

Bell, Charles G., ed. 1973. *Growth and Change: A Reader in Political Socialization*. Encino, CA: Dickenson.

Bennett, Linda L.M., and Stephen E. Bennett. 1989. "Enduring Gender Differences in Political Interest: The Impact of Socialization and Political Dispositions." *American Politics Quarterly* 17 (January): 105-122.

Bennett, Linda L.M., and Stephen E. Bennett. 1990. *Living with Leviathan: Americans Coming to Terms with Big Government*. Lawrence, KS: University Press of Kansas.

Bennett, Stephen E. 1986. *Apathy in America*, 1960-1984. Dobbs Ferry, NY: Transnational.

Bennett, Stephen E. 1997. "Why Young Americans Hate Politics, and What We Should Do About It." *PS: Political Science and Politics* 30 (March): 47-53.

Bennett, Stephen E. 1998. "Young Americans' Indifference to Media Coverage of Public Affairs." *PS: Political Science and Politics* 31 (September): 535-541.

Brokaw, Tom. 1998. *The Greatest Generation*. New York: Random House.

Campbell, Angus, Philip E. Converse, Warren E. Miller, and Donald E. Stokes. 1960. *The American Voter*. New York: Wiley.

Cannon, Angie, and Carolyn Kleiner. 2000. "Teens Get Real: Adolescents Get A

Bad Rap Today, But Many Are Choosing an Unfamiliar Route: Doing Good." *US News & World Report* (April 17): 46-55.

Collier, Peter, and David Horowitz. 1989. *Destructive Generation: Second Thoughts about the '60s*. New York: Summit.

Conover, Pamela Johnston. 1991. "Political Socialization: Where's the Politics?" In *Political Science: Looking to the Future*, William Crotty, ed. Volume 3. Evanston, IL: Northwestern University Press.

Converse, Philip E., with Richard G. Niemi. 1971. "Non-voting Among Young Adults in the United States." In *Political Parties and Political Behavior*, William J. Crotty, Donald S. Freeman, and Douglas S. Gatlin, eds. Second Edition. Boston: Allyn & Bacon.

Conway, M. Margaret. 2000. *Political Participation in the United States*. Third Edition. Washington, DC: Congressional Quarterly Press.

Craig, Stephen, and Stephen E. Bennett, eds. 1997. *After the Boom: The Politics of Generation X*. Lanham, MD: Rowman & Littlefield.

Dahl, Robert A. 1998. *On Democracy*. New Haven, CT: Yale University Press.

Delli Carpini, Michael X. 1986. *Stability and Change in American Politics: The Coming of Age of the Generation of the 1960s*. New York: New York University Press.

Delli Carpini, Michael X., and Scott Keeter. 1996. *What Americans Know about Politics, and Why It Matters*. New Haven, CT: Yale University Press.

Dennis, Jack, ed. 1973. *Socialization to Politics*. New York: Wiley.

Doppelt, Jack C., and Ellen Shearer. 1999. *Nonvoters: America's No-Shows*. Thousand Oaks, CA: Sage.

Easton, David, and Jack W. Dennis. 1969. *Children in the Political System: Origins of Political Legitimacy*. New York: McGraw-Hill.

Ehrlich, Thomas. 1998. "Civic Education: Lessons Learned." *PS: Political Science and Politics* 32 (June): 245-250.

Feuer, Lewis S. 1969. *The Conflict of Generations: The Character and Significance of Student Movements*. New York: Basic.

Flacks, Richard. 1971. *Youth and Social Change*. Chicago: Markham.

Gallup, George, and Alec Gallup. 2000. "American Teens Need a History Lesson: Boys More Accurate than Girls." *Gallup News Service*. Available at <http://www.gallup.com/poll/index.asp> (May 5).

Glenn, Norval D. 1977. *Cohort Analysis*. Sage University Paper series on Quantitative Applications in the Social Sciences, series no. 07-007. Beverly Hills, CA: Sage.

Glenn, Norval D. 1994. "Television Watching, Newspaper Reading, and Cohort Differences in Verbal Ability." *Sociology of Education* 67 (July): 216-230.

Glenn, Norval D., and Michael Grimes. 1968. "Aging, Voting, and Political Interest." *American Sociological Review* 33 (August): 563-575.

Greenstein, Fred I. 1969. *Children and Politics*. Revised Edition. New Haven, CT: Yale University Press.

Hess, Robert D., and Judith V. Torney. 1967. *The Development of Political Attitudes in Children*. Chicago: Aldine.

Hine, Thomas. 1999. *The Rise and Fall of the American Teenager*. New York: Avon.

Janowitz, Morris. 1983. *The Reconstruction of Patriotism: Education for Civic Consciousness*. Chicago: University of Chicago Press.

Jaros, Dean. 1973. *Socialization to Politics*. New York: Praeger.

Jennings, M. Kent. 1979. "Another Look at the Life Cycle and Political Participation." *American Journal of Political Science* 23 (November): 755-771.

Jennings, M. Kent. 1996. "Political Knowledge Over Time and Across Generations." *Public Opinion Quarterly* 60 (Summer): 228-252.

Jennings, M. Kent, and Richard G. Niemi. 1974. *The Political Character of Adolescence: The Influence of Families and Schools*. Princeton, NJ: Princeton University Press.

Jennings, M. Kent, and Richard G. Niemi. 1981. *Generations and Politics: A Panel Study of Young Adults and Their Parents*. Princeton, NJ: Princeton University Press.

Kinder, Donald R., and David O. Sears. 1985. "Public Opinion and Political Action." In *Handbook of Social Psychology*, Gardner Lindzey and Elliot Aronson, eds. Third Edition. Volume 2. New York: Random House.

Kleiner, Carolyn, and Mary Lord. 1999. "The Cheating Game: 'Everyone's Doing It,' from Grade School to Graduate School." *U.S. News & World Report* (November 17): 54-66.

Kleppner, Paul. 1982. *Who Voted? The Dynamics of Electoral Turnout, 1870-1980*. New York: Praeger.

Langton, Kenneth P. 1969. *Political Socialization*. New York: Oxford University Press.

Langton, Kenneth P., and M. Kent Jennings. 1968. "Political Socialization and the High School Civics Curriculum in the United States." *American Political Science Review* 62 (September): 852-867.

Leonard, Stephen T. 1999. "'Pure Futility and Waste': Academic Political Science and Civic Education." *PS: Political Science and Politics* 32 (December): 749-754.

Light, Paul C. 1988. *Baby Boomers*. New York: Norton.

Littwin, Susan. 1986. *The Postponed Generation: Why American Youth Are Growing Up Later*. New York: Morrow.

Lutkus, Anthony et al. 1999. *NAEP 1998 Civics Report Card for the Nation*. Washington, DC: U.S. Department of Education.

MacPherson, Myra. 1984. *Long Time Passing: Vietnam and the Haunted Generation*. Garden City, NY: Doubleday.

Mann, Sheilah. 1999. "What the Survey of American College Freshmen Tells Us About Their Interest in Politics and Political Science." *PS: Political Science and Politics* 32 (December): 749-754.

Mannheim, Karl. [1928] 1952. "The Problem of Generations." In *Essays on the Sociology of Knowledge*, Paul Kecskemeti, ed. London: Routledge & Kegan Paul.

Morin, Richard. 2000. "What Americans Think: Don't Know Much about History." *The Washington Post National Weekly Edition*. (April 17): 34.

National Association of Secretaries of State. 1998. *New Millennium Project, Part I: American Youth Attitudes on Politics, Citizenship, Government and Voting.* Lexington, KY: National Association of Secretaries of State.

National Commission on Civic Renewal. 1998. *A Nation of Spectators: How Civic Disengagement Weakens America and What We Can Do About It.* College Park: Institute for Philosophy and Public Policy, University of Maryland.

Niemi, Richard G. 1974. *How Family Members Perceive Each Other: Political and Social Attitudes in Two Generations.* New Haven, CT: Yale University Press.

Niemi, Richard G., et al., eds. 1974. *The Politics of Future Citizens: New Dimensions in the Political Socialization of Children.* San Francisco: Jossey-Bass.

Niemi, Richard G., and Jane Junn. 1998. *Civic Education: What Makes Students Learn.* New Haven, CT: Yale University Press.

Orum, Anthony, ed. 1972. *The Seeds of Politics: Youth and Politics in America.* Englewood Cliffs, NJ: Prentice-Hall.

People for the American Way. 1989. *Democracy's Next Generation: A Study of Youth and Teachers.* Washington, DC: People for the American Way.

Pomper, Gerald M. 1988. *Voters, Elections, and Parties: The Practice of Democratic Theory.* New Brunswick, NJ: Transaction.

Putnam, Robert D. 1995a. "Bowling Alone: America's Declining Social Capital." *Journal of Democracy* 6 (January): 65-78.

Putnam, Robert D. 1995b. "Tuning In, Tuning Out: The Strange Disappearance of Social Capital in America." *PS: Political Science and Politics* 28 (December): 664-683.

Rahn, Wendy M. 1998. "Generations and American National Identity: A Data Essay." Paper presented at The Annenberg Center's "Communication in the Future of Democracy Workshop." Washington, DC (April 20).

Rahn, Wendy M., and John E. Transue. 1998. "Social Trust and Value Change: The Decline of Social Capital in American Youth, 1976-1995." *Political Psychology* 19 (September): 545-565.

Renshon, Stanley Allen, ed. 1977. *Handbook of Political Socialization: Theory and Research.* New York: Free Press.

Sax, Linda J., Alexander W. Astin, William S. Korn, and Kathryn M. Mahoney. 1998. *The American Freshman: National Norms for Fall 1998.* Los Angeles: Higher Education Research Institute, Graduate School of Education & Information Studies, University of California, Los Angeles.

Sax, Linda J., Alexander W. Astin, William S. Korn, and Kathryn M. Mahoney. 1999. *The American Freshman: National Norms for Fall 1999.* Los Angeles: Higher Education Research Institute, Graduate School of Education & Information Studies, University of California, Los Angeles.

Schachter, Hindy Lauer. 1998. "Civic Education: Three Early American Political Science Association Committees and Their Relevance to Our Times." *PS: Political Science and Politics* 31 (September): 631-635.

Schneider, Barbara, and David Stevenson. 1999. *The Ambitious Generation: America's Teenagers, Motivated but Directionless.* New Haven, CT: Yale University Press.

Schwartz, David C., and Sandra Kenyon Schwartz, eds. 1975. *New Directions in Political Socialization.* New York: Free Press.

Searing, Donald D., James J. Schwartz, and Alfred E. Lind. 1973. "The Structuring Principle: Political Socialization and Belief Systems." *American Political Science Review* 67 (June): 415-432.

Searing, Donald G., George Wright, and George Rabinowitz. 1976. "The Primacy Principle: Attitude Change and Political Socialization." *British Journal of Political Science* 6 (January): 83-113.

Sears, David O. 1975. "Political Socialization." In *Handbook of Political Science,* Fred I. Greenstein and Nelson W. Polsby, eds. Volume 2. Reading, MA: Addison-Wesley.

Sigel, Roberta, ed. 1965. "Political Socialization: Its Role in the Political Process." *The Annals of the American Academy of Political and Social Science* 361 (September).

Sigel, Roberta, ed. 1969. *Learning about Politics: A Reader in Political Socialization.* New York: Random House.

Sigel, Roberta, and Marilyn B. Hoskin. 1981. *The Political Involvement of Adolescents.* New Brunswick, NJ: Rutgers University Press.

Squire, Peverill, Raymond E. Wolfinger, and David P. Glass. 1987. "Residential Mobility and Voter Turnout." *American Political Science Review* 81 (March): 45-65.

Starr, Jerold M. 1986. "American Youth in the 1980s." *Youth and Society* 17 (June): 323-345.

Strauss, William, and Neil Howe. 1997. *The Fourth Turning: An American Prophecy.* New York: Broadway.

"Students Weak on Civics." *The Cincinnati Enquirer,* November 19, 1999, A2.

Thau, Richard, and Robert M. Eisinger. 2000. "Younger Voters Get Short Shrift." *USA Today* (April 26): 17A.

Teixeira, Ruy A. 1992. *The Disappearing American Voter.* Washington, DC: Brookings.

*Times Mirror.* 1990. "The Age of Indifference: A Study of Young Americans and How They View the News." Washington, DC: *Times Mirror* Center for The People & The Press (June 28).

Van Deth, Jan W. 1990. "Political Interest." In *Continuities in Political Action,* M. Kent Jennings, Jan W. Van Deth, et al., eds. Berlin: de Gruyter.

"Vanishing Voter." 2000. "Election Apathy Pervasive among Young Adults." Cambridge, MA: The Joan Shorenstein Center, John F. Kennedy School of Government, Harvard University. Available at <http://www.vanishing voter.org> (May 12).

Verba, Sidney, Kay Lehman Schlozman, and Henry E. Brady. 1995. *Voice and Equality: Civic Voluntarism in American Politics.* Cambridge, MA: Harvard University Press.

Wolfinger, Raymond E., and Steven J. Rosenstone. 1980. *Who Votes?* New Haven, CT: Yale University Press.

# 3

# Service Learning and Civic Education

## *Richard M. Battistoni*

*Over the course of this semester I have become a citizen of New Brunswick. It could be argued that I was a citizen here well before registering for the course, but I did not feel as if I were one. Having taken the course, I now know why I felt as I did. A citizen must play an active role in his or her community. A citizen must work for change, and never accept the status quo – things can always be better. I am now aware of what is happening around me. . . . I now see the city differently. I'm no longer scared walking to [my service site] – far from it. I feel like I know that small portion of the city now. Now when I pass people in the street, some say hello to me, and call me by name. Through my work I've gotten to know individual people, and they've gotten to know me. I enjoy my community service. It has opened my eyes as to the role I play as a citizen in my community.*

The above quote is from a college student, but the sentiment underlying it just as easily could come from a high school or middle-school student. My experience with service-learning programs at all levels has been that when democratic citizenship is at the foundation of a community-based service experience, students can come away with a better and more critical understanding of their communities and their own roles as citizens in them. My experience has also taught me, however, that the connection between service and civic education is not automatic. Without careful consideration of the substantive issues addressed and the pedagogical strategies employed, students involved in service-learning activities may come away as (or more) civically disengaged (as the evidence suggests most are) than they were before participating in service-learning activities.

## Challenges and Opportunities of Civic Education through Service Learning

This chapter makes the case for service learning as an effective means to a more engaged and knowledgeable citizenry, but only if undertaken with regard to particular political objectives of democracy. This argument begins with the premise that democratic civic and political learning are not innate, but the result of conscious and ongoing work by educators. This premise – argued by Thomas Jefferson, John Adams, and George Washington at the founding of the American republic, Alexis de Tocqueville, Walt Whitman, and Horace Mann in the nineteenth century, and John Dewey, Hannah Arendt, and Benjamin Barber in the twentieth century – is that the rights, benefits, and structural processes of democracy are incomplete, and cannot be sustained without the formation of civic character and a rich civic culture. Attention to this premise is especially important given our free market economy and private sphere of life, which can readily entice citizens of a liberal democracy away from a vigorous civic life in the public sphere and toward individual concern for personal wealth and happiness.

Democracy requires constant attention. Those who struggle for freedom need to learn that heavy burdens and responsibilities go with it. As Jean-Jacques Rousseau, the political theorist of the eighteenth century who inspired some of the earliest democratic revolutions in the Western world, once wrote: "Freedom is a food that is easy to swallow but hard to digest" (Rousseau [1772] 1972, 29). Freedom is hard work that must be done by all of us, on a daily basis. Democratic citizenship and the arts of self-government are not things we know innately. Like reading, writing, and mathematics, they are qualities acquired through the learning process. As John Dewey, the great twentieth-century philosopher of democracy and democratic experiential education, reminds us: "Democracy has to be born anew every generation, and education is the midwife" (quoted in Morse 1990, 3).

It has been a fundamental mission of public schooling in the United States to train youth in the theory and practice of democratic citizenship, to form the civic character of young people (Cremin 1961). Educational institutions are no less important today as the best institution available to society as a whole to fulfill this civic mission. Most civic qualities cannot be learned in private spheres like the family or workplaces, and while these places and others, such as churches, voluntary associations, and the media all play roles in young people's civic development, it is schools that provide that unique environment to balance the development of individuality, autonomy, confidence, and knowledge with the strengthening of the public self through dialogue (including dialogue with adults), decision making, and cooperative learning.

Obviously, if we were confident that schools performed this function, there would not be the kind of concern over young people's civic disengagement so clearly portrayed in Stephen Bennett's chapter in this book. "Crisis" as it is so often applied to American education, is a rash word; nonetheless, there obviously has been erosion of our democratic civic culture and the failure of our educational institutions to develop engaged citizens.

Over the past decade, many schools have attempted to solve the problem of civic education through programs that place students in community-based service activities. The National Center for Education Statistics reports that "83 percent of high schools offer community-service opportunities to their students, compared with 27 percent in 1984" (West-heimer & Kahne 2000). Two years ago, the National Commission on Civic Renewal's report affirmed this strategy:

> We believe that our schools should foster the knowledge, skills, and virtues our young people need to become good democratic  citizens [and] are impressed with the ways in which well-designed community work care-fully linked to classroom reflection can enhance the civic education of stu-dents. (National Commission on Civic Renewal 1998)

Beyond the good intentions of school administrators and national com-missions, a growing body of evidence – from political scientists practicing community-based learning – strongly suggests that when accompanied by proper preparation and adequate academic reflection, service learning can be a potent civic educator (Farr 1997; Guarasci 1997; Markus et al. 1993; Mendel-Reyes 1997; Rimmerman 1997; Walker 2000). Of course, I have often made this claim that citizenship education can be a powerful foundation and outcome for service learning, based on my experiences teaching courses on three different urban campuses. My students' own reflections – as evidenced in the excerpt at the beginning of this chapter and those scattered throughout it – indicate that a community service experience connected to courses centered on education for democratic cit-izenship can achieve the goal of educating young people about their responsibilities in a democratic society, allowing them to think about what it means to be a part of the multiple communities in which they find themselves (Battistoni 1997a).

Having praised community service as a potent civic educator, a few warnings are in order. The first and foremost one lies in the powerful cri-tique of community service as being apolitical. After all, many students actively involved in community service say that they have chosen service as an antidote to politics. The annual Higher Education Research Insti-tute's "Freshman Survey" in 1999 reported record lows for almost all measures of political interest or involvement, coupled with a record of over 75 percent reporting that they had done community service in their senior year of high school (Sax et al. 1999). The most recent survey com-

missioned by the National Association of Secretaries of State (NASS) of
15-24 year-olds confirms the considerable disaffection from political life
and electoral politics among younger Americans and suggests that as
more young people volunteer, fewer see any connection between service
and political engagement, which continues to rank low in importance in
young people's lives (National Association of Secretaries of State 1999).
Harry Boyte, perhaps the most trenchant of critics, has written that "community service is not a cure for young people's political apathy" primarily because "it teaches little about the arts of participation in public life"
(Boyte 1991, 765).

A second, related *caveat* lies in the pedagogical understanding that civic
learning does not automatically happen from a community service experience. Merely sending students out to do any kind of service in communities, with little opportunity for preparation or reflection, may indeed
reinforce ingrained attitudes in students, toward people as well as politics
(but for a qualified dissent, see Campbell 2000). As John Dewey understood, the "discipline of experience" by itself may even be "miseduca-
tive," and therefore must always be subjected "to the tests of intelligent
development and direction" (Dewey 1938, 89-90). A recent comprehensive
study of pre-college service-learning programs reported chilling findings
that only a few programs are structured to make connections between
community service and the values and skills necessary for effective democratic citizenship, and the faculty and staff involved with these programs
cannot agree on what a good citizen does (Westheimer and Kahne 2000).

To be effective, we must constantly keep civic learning outcomes in
mind as we design service-learning courses and programs. This raises the
question: what do we mean by "civic education?" In response, we need to
distinguish between substantive, conceptual frameworks for civic education, and the complement of skills and knowledge that a person should
possess to be an effective citizen. The conceptual question is critical, yet
sticky, wrapped up in issues surrounding fundamental values, lan-
guage/definitions, and tensions between personal or local and national
identities. Recent calls – as exhibited in national studies – for educators to
re-engage students as citizens generally assume a unified language of
commonwealth, obscuring the realities and challenges of pluralism, both
of values and identity. Students today are often suspicious of this language, and do not see any inherent connection between their service
(often a local identity) and their role as citizens (a national identity, if a
positive identity at all). This can become complicated by the very use of
the language of citizenship applied to matters that have little to do with
civic education. In California, for example, public schools still give "citizenship" grades on report cards based on a students' neatness, politeness,

and passive obedience to school rules; moreover, "citizenship" as a legal status places many teachers in the role of Immigration and Naturalization Service agent.

Even those political and social scientists intent on substituting a different civic language create problems by insisting on a particular (and singular) language or conceptual approach to citizenship and civic education. If only we would endorse one perspective, so the argument goes, whether it be "communitarianism" (Etzoni 1993), "public work" (Boyte & Kari 1996; Hildreth 2000), "social capital" (Putnam 1993; 1995), or "strong democracy" (Barber 1984; 1998), we could more easily revitalize democratic civic practice in America. We need, however, to be open to a greater diversity of perspectives about what it means to be a democratic citizen. While political and other social scientists have a rich tradition and language around concepts like democracy, citizenship, community, political participation, civil society, and public affairs, we obviously do not have a lock on these concepts, and given the evidence of declining political participation, we may not be communicating it very effectively or in a way that resonates with students.

The more we engage in narrow or rhetorical definitions of service and citizenship, the more we may turn away young people. This calls at once for all disciplines, which may have equally effective conceptual frameworks, to join into the discourse around a multidisciplinary civic education. To paraphrase a wonderful statement made by Vaclav Havel in one of his first New Year's Addresses to his nation, the public problems we face as a people are such that require the collaboration of "well-rounded people," those informed by a variety of perspectives and conceptual frameworks (Havel 1997, 9).

We must make room in our practices and in our curriculum for conversations where students name for themselves what it is they are doing and its connections to community, citizenship, and democratic politics (Morton & Battistoni 1995). In my experience, this means beginning with students' motivations, language, and philosophies around service, all of which may be private or apolitical, and using politically oriented texts or materials to determine whether a more civic or public language resonates with their aspirations (Battistoni 1997a; Walker 2000). This may seem like a monumental challenge, but the corresponding opportunity for educators is that the service-learning/civic education agenda may align itself with other contemporary agendas in education, from problem-centered learning to diversity and multiculturalism, to non-service-based experiential learning, to structural school reform or alternative (for example, outcomes- or competency-based) assessment.

But beyond the conceptual framework for understanding what it

means to be a citizen in a democracy, we must also be able to make connections between service learning and the development of students' concrete civic skills. In looking at central skills necessary for effective
citizenship, I will focus on three general areas: intellectual understanding,
communication and public problem solving, and the development of civic
judgment and imagination.

## Intellectual Understanding

As with other areas of the curriculum, intellectual understanding
comes first in civic education. In 1893, for example, a "Committee of Ten"
leading American educators produced a report which said the chief purpose of education was "to train the mind." The main thrust of effective
education at all levels is cognitive development.

The "thinking citizen" is certainly an important aim of civic education.
We want to develop citizens who can use a variety of methods, theories,
and models to examine the world and evaluate facts to reach conclusions.

Service learning can enhance the development of students' critical
thinking skills, and experiences in the community can reveal challenges to
their cognitive assumptions on human nature, society, and justice. Students' ability to analyze critically is enhanced by confronting academic
ideas and theories with the actual realities in the world surrounding
them. For example, I have placed students in service experiences to work
with guests in homeless shelters, and they have reported such positive
outcomes as their capacity to put a face on "the poor" and to test theories
about poverty, public policy, and democracy against actual observations
and the real-life stories of those with whom they interacted in the shelters.

## Communication and Problem Solving

Intellectual understanding, while essential to democratic citizenship,
must be accompanied by "participation skills" – those of communication
and problem solving – that can be developed through service learning.
Alexis de Tocqueville laid out clearly the argument for participation in
community-based organizations as essential to maintain democratic institutions and to educate people for citizenship. He argued that in democracies, "All the citizens are independent and feeble; they can do hardly
anything by themselves, and none of them can oblige [others] to lend
their assistance. They all therefore become powerless if they do not learn
voluntarily to help one another." Participation in civic associations edu-
cates people to overcome this powerlessness and isolation, since through
this participation members of associations learn "the art of pursuing in

common the object of their common desires" and of "proposing a common object for the exertions of a great many and inducing them voluntarily to pursue it" (Tocqueville [1835] 1945, 115). More recently, Robert Putnam (1995, 2000) has echoed Tocqueville's argument, lamenting the decline in voluntary associations and the subsequent loss of "social capital," the foundation of our democracy.

To be effective, students' participation in community-based organizations should be accompanied by educational efforts aimed at "thickening those bonds of connectedness" formed by such participation with adults in civic associations (Campbell 2000). For example, students doing service work in a community-based organization can be given academic assignments that require them to learn more about the organization's operation and interactions with the community and with government (including interviews with staff and board members), as a way of deepening their understanding of the role of civic or not-for-profit organizations in American public life.

Communication skills are essential to effective civic participation. In addition to clear thinking about public matters, democratic citizenship involves the communication of our thoughts and actions, both vertically, to our leaders and representatives, and horizontally, to our fellow citizens. Speech, argument, and persuasive communication are all important elements of democratic literacy.

Perhaps even more important is the lost art of listening. In a democracy, citizens need to be able to listen to each other, to understand the places and interests of others in the community, and to achieve compromises and solve problems when conflict occurs. The overriding images of our democratic culture tend to involve talkers; great communicators like Thomas Jefferson, Daniel Webster, Martin Luther King, and Ronald Reagan; representatives giving speeches or talking on C-SPAN; or lawyers persuasively arguing in the courtroom. Perhaps the truer image of democracy exists on the other side of the courtroom, among the members of the jury, both listening to the arguments and testimony and to each other in deliberation. An effective congressional representative delivers persuasive speeches on the House floor, yet he or she also listens carefully to constituents at public hearings. Effective civic education must involve the development of the ability to listen as part of communication skills.

Service-learning programs that employ appropriate and varied reflective strategies heighten students' communicative abilities. Through reflecting on their service experiences, students are called upon to give an account of themselves and their thoughts in classroom discussions, in oral or artistic presentations, and in their writings (Battistoni 1997a, 95-96). In addition, the community service experience itself can teach students to listen to the stories and needs of others. When tutoring, visiting an elderly person, serving overnight in a homeless shelter, or doing an oral history, our students learn, in a tangible way, the art of listening. But once again, for these skills to be most effectively developed, time and effort must be spent in structuring both the service experience and that of the classroom to maximize student dialogue and listening opportunities.

The other "participation skill" I stress is the ability to identify and solve public problems. Too often community-service and service-learning programs overemphasize the service activity, leading students to conclude that their service is both the problem (what service to perform, how to organize it) and the solution (to larger social problems). Consider the infamous example of the student who reported that her service experience was so meaningful that she hoped her children would have the opportunity to work in homeless shelters. This example reminds us that service is not an end in itself (Chi 1999, 227). Only when service leads students to examine the underlying issues beneath their community work to identify concerns/problems, and then to explore with fellow citizens possible solutions to these public problems, have we done our best to make service an education for democratic citizenship. A former student of mine made this point clearly in a written assignment:

> Community service is nothing new to me. I've always done it whole-heartedly and thought of it as something useful and necessary. However, [in this class] I began to realize that helping individuals is only part of the solution. The scope of the problem was wider social problems, economic problems, social neglect and apathy, political neglect; and without addressing these, nothing could fix the problems individuals face.

As an example of the kind of curricular assignment that would support public problem solving, I have asked students serving at an organization or school to identify the "central public problem" to which the organization/service site has been developed to respond, to state the problem, and to investigate the causes and consequences of it, and the possible responses to it. What I have found is that a public problem statement/research assignment serves to get students thinking about the larger political and policy dimensions of the service they are doing, and enhances their critical thinking and imagining skills. I have seen students come to the jarring realization that their identification of the public problem, which the organization is designed to address, differs from the organization's own definition of the central problem. Other students have done research that reveals alternative approaches to tackling the problem from those taken by the organization in which they are serving, also something that promotes the kinds of critical civic skills we need to engender in students. But I am not alone in thinking this way: the Westheimer and Kahne study (cited above) found "compelling evidence that when service experiences are combined with rigorous analysis or related social issues, students do develop attitudes, skills, and knowledge necessary to respond in productive ways."

Problem solving can go beyond the content or assignments in a service-learning class. In my experience, students have learned public problem-solving skills in the context of working together to make their service placement more meaningful and/or more aligned with their abilities and interests. In countless situations, I have witnessed students, working in teams, having to work through problems at their service sites, problems of organization, effective use of their time, or creative programming. For example, students working in an after-school program complained about their relationships with site staff and their "not being effectively used." They met with the program director and developed an alternative structure that allowed them to interact more with program staff and plan after-school activities of their own for the children. This experience in problem solving at their community service site enhanced not only their work that semester, but also their civic capacity. Other students have learned similar lessons about problem solving through "participant observation," – watching others at their placement sites work together to solve common concerns. One of my students wrote:

> Service allows you to work closely with people towards a common, respectable goal. When a group works together towards a common good, it inevitably becomes closer, even if the group is diverse. Working at [my service site], I've seen people of all ages, all races, religions and financial status befriend each other and work successfully together.

Both the service activities and the service-learning program should be organized so that public problem solving will be one of the outcomes. This is best done by organizing students into service "teams" (where collaborative learning pedagogies can be employed), as opposed to individual placements, and by giving students an active role in the design and structure of the school's service-learning program itself (Barber & Battistoni 1993; Battistoni 1997; Wade 1997).

## Civic Judgment and Imagination

A service-learning program aimed at civic education should develop students' civic dispositions associated with public judgment and imagination. Civic judgment is the ability to apply publicly defendable moral standards to the actual life and history of a community. A citizenship-oriented service-learning program can develop capacities for public judgment, because the practical experience students gain through their community involvement allows them to set and reset their standards of judgment, and it may cause them to modify their political judgments in reaction to the world they observe and the people with whom they interact. Two of my students wrote:

> I think this class has really opened a lot of people's eyes to what they are like, and what their communities are like. I also think it has made people more aware of the different perspectives we all have. It is an incredible feeling to be able to see things from a different perspective. I learned a lot more about the views which I differ from. And in fact I have changed some of my previous beliefs after reading, hearing, and experiencing the "other side."

These two excerpts suggest that students emerge from a quality service-learning experience more open and tolerant (see Walt Whitman Center, 1996, for further evidence with respect to religious and racial tolerance). But beyond enhancing civic dispositions like openness and toleration, service learning can encourage the crucial civic competence of imagination, which involves the ability to think creatively about public problems. Moreover, to put oneself truly in the place of others requires more than mere tolerance; it requires imagination. Imagination is also present in the ability to project and embrace a vision for the future, to think about oneself and one's community in ways not tied to the past, to dream things that never were and say, "Why not?"– as George Bernard Shaw put it. Students imaginative abilities can be enhanced through service learning by enlarging their sense of who they are and enabling them to use their imagination to join together in working toward a common goal with people who have different backgrounds, values, and life stories.

## Four Constituents of Civic Education through Service Learning

I have tried to make a case for service learning as a vehicle to civic education. A properly designed service experience can be civically transformative, because students are immersed in a community setting, potentially working with an organization or a school on an issue of public dimensions, working with people coming from different backgrounds or with different interests in the issue. It offers, in a way that classrooms or traditional texts cannot, a tangible context for exploring and understanding the very issues of public concern that give rise to the needs for community service. Under optimal conditions, experiential education in the form of service learning is a powerful pedagogy that reaches beyond teaching and learning to recognize that "democracy is a learned activity and that active participation in the life of a community is a bridge to citizenship" (Saltmarsh & Hollander 2000). But what are the optimal conditions under which service learning can translate into civic learning? Here, both substantively and strategically, it is most useful to regard the community service connected to any civic education-oriented learning as one of the central "texts" (for a good definition of "service as text," see Morton 1996). The metaphor of "service as text" creates its own set of conditions, for each of the four constituents of any well-grounded service-learning program: students, faculty, school program as a whole, and community partners. I will look at each in turn.

**Students**. For service learning to work optimally as a vehicle for civic education, students need to dig deeper in their reflection on the service experience, beyond how they feel or what they are doing or the charitable motivations behind what they are doing to the "civic" or "public" dimensions of their work. This means that they need to critically examine their experience as they would any other "text" in a classroom setting. This is something that can be difficult for students, many of whom want to do service to avoid critically analyzing or reflecting, particularly in terms of "civic awareness" or "democratic practice." They want to act, to make an immediate difference. Fighting this inclination is important, because in addition to being primarily apolitical in their orientation to service, young people also tend to be anti-institutional. Many of the young people I work with initially view service as a direct, and therefore preferable, form of intervention into a problem or situation. They are not inclined to consider the organizational structures or imperatives (and therefore, the power structures) within which all citizens must work. And yet, without considering the organizational "text" and "context" of their service work, they will certainly be less effective citizens (Hildreth 2000).

**Faculty**. Like students, faculty need to regard the service experience as a "civic text," with all that encompasses. This means that both the process and the substance of the service experience needs to be pre-examined to make sure it can be "mined" for civic themes. I am a firm believer that not just any service experience will do if one seeks democratic civic learning outcomes. As with any text, faculty should choose the kind of service attached to such a course intentionally, with a view to enhancing the political content of the course. Opportunities for students to work in political campaigns or with political parties, with public agencies, or in community organizing or community development might be the most conducive to drawing forth civic lessons from students. But there are also examples – like the Public Achievement program featured in this monograph, the Constitutional Rights Foundation's "Project ACT" (Clark et al. 1997), or my "civic organizational research" project mentioned above – where service that is not directly "political" can offer rich civic learning opportunities. Beyond the selection of "politically rich" community-based service experiences, faculty should structure their courses more consciously to allow for structured opportunities for students to critically reflect upon the political aspects of the "text" that is their service work, as well as the civic nature of the other, written "texts." Additionally, faculty using a community-based experience as a "text" need to be familiar with the lived service text, as they would any written text, which calls for greater engagement in the community partnership than we typically see in service learning – at least understanding the dimensions and complexities of students' service, so as to be able to ask the right (for example, civically oriented) questions in class or in written assignments. Finally, teachers incorporating community service into a "civic education" curriculum need to pay attention to their pedagogy, making sure that it enhances democratic civic practice (for a more extensive discussion, see Battistoni 1996).

**The School/Program as a Whole**. I have already spoken about the need to have students involved in the design and management of the school's service-learning program as a whole. Students should play an active role in planning the program and serve as leaders in it not only because students have good ideas and can recruit and organize other students, but also because active participation in service learning can help students learn the lessons of democracy (for a more extensive argument, see Battistoni 1996). This argument also applies to giving students greater involvement in school-wide decisions more generally. In addition, an emphasis on education for democratic citizenship should cause any school to reexamine its relationship with the larger community. This begs the question: does the school as a whole act as a good *institutional* citizen in the larger community? Does it approach the community as a "partner in education" rather than a set of clients to be served? Partnership underscores interdependence and helps create an understanding of community – not as those with problems but as the group to which we all belong. The community comes to be seen as "text," and neighborhoods reciprocally gain the opportunity to reclaim their schools as centers of the community (Lappe & Dubois 1994). At the very least, the school must exhibit a commitment to provide a positive orientation to the community and to the particular organization with which the students are working. This allows students as well as community partners to see the civic value in what is going on.

**Community Partners**. Too often I have seen service-learning programs let community partners off the hook so to speak. They make sure the community's need is articulated in setting up the service activity, but they basically treat the organization as a "placement site," rather than as a real partner in education. And many community partners have neither the time nor the interest to serve as co-civic educators for that might require understanding the learning outcomes sought by the faculty/students and trying to meet those substantive interests. Or it might require opening themselves up to questioning, like whether the "expert-client" nature of the organization's operation is in keeping with its democratic or civic mission, or whether this community-based organization – literally as well as figuratively – really represents the community being served. This kind of commitment on the part of community partners is not an easy thing to ask for. But if service learning is indeed reciprocal, we have to hold all constituents – including community-based ones – accountable to the mutual interests in long-term collaboration.

## Concluding Thoughts

Service learning can be a particularly effective method of civic education, if we pay attention to the democratic political outcomes we seek in the design of our programs, curriculum, and pedagogy. "Paying attention" in the specific ways I suggest may seem like a lot to ask of all involved. At the very least, it means paying attention to the two critical "warnings" or conditions discussed above.

The first is my plea to incorporate a diversity of perspectives about what it means to be a "democratic citizen." Narrow or rhetorical definitions of service and citizenship are inadequate to the task of inviting into a public dialogue and public life the people, especially young people, who have walked away. In our thinking about the relationship between the individual self and the community, we need to draw upon all perspectives, including those of young people themselves. And we must look closely at the kinds of skills young people need for effective citizenship – some of which I've suggested above – and the connection of these skills to service-learning content and pedagogy. All of this argues in addition for new ways to evaluate or measure the "civic impact" of participation in service learning.

Secondly, we must keep in mind my earlier point that service alone does not automatically lead to engaged citizenship; only if we consciously construct our programs with the education of democratic citizens (broadly understood) in mind can service learning be one of the vehicles by which we reinvigorate our rapidly deteriorating public life. I have attempted here to make suggestions about how we might rethink our practices in line with outcomes focused on civic engagement and democracy. These suggestions about "optimal conditions" may be difficult to achieve. But if we truly care about the civic and democratic outcomes of our service-learning practices, there is no other way to get there but to intentionally rearrange our practices with these outcomes fully in mind.

## References

Barber, Benjamin R. 1984. *Strong Democracy*. Berkeley, CA: University of California Press.

Barber, Benjamin R. 1998. *A Passion for Democracy*. Princeton, NJ: Princeton University Press.

Barber, Benjamin R., and Richard M. Battistoni. 1993. "A Season of Service: Introducing Service Learning into the Liberal Arts Curriculum." *PS: Political Science & Politics* 26 (June): 235-240.

Battistoni, Richard M. 1997. "Service-Learning in a Democratic Society: Essential Practices for K-12 Programs." *Community Service-Learning: A Guide to Including Service in the Public School Curriculum*. Albany, NY: SUNY Press.

Battistoni, Richard M. 1997a. "Service Learning as Civic Learning: Lessons We Can Learn From Our Students." In *Education for Citizenship: Ideas and Innovations in Political Learning*, Grant Reeher and Joseph Cammarano, eds. Lanham, MD: Rowman & Littlefield Publishers.

Boyte, Harry C. 1991. "Community Service and Civic Education." *Phi Delta Kappan* 72 (June): 765-767.

Boyte, Harry C., and Nancy N. Kari. 1996. *Building America: The Democratic Promise of Public Work*. Philadelphia: Temple University Press.

Campbell, David E. 2000. "Social Capital and Service Learning." *PS: Political Science and Politics*. 33 (September): 641-646.

Chi, Bernadette. 1999. "What's Wrong with This Picture?" In *Education for Democracy*, Benjamin R. Barber and Richard M. Battistoni, eds. Des Moines, IA: Kendall/Hunt Publishing.

Clark, Todd, Marshall Croddy, William Hayes, and Susan Philips. 1997. "Service Learning as Civic Participation." *Theory into Practice*. 36 (Summer): 164-169.

Cremin, Lawrence. 1961. *The Transformation of the School: Progressivism in American Education*. New York: Alfred A. Knopf.

Dewey, John. 1938. *Experience and Education*. New York: Macmillan.

Etzioni, Amitai. 1993. *The Spirit of Community: Rights, Responsibilities, and the Communitarian Agenda*. New York: Crown Publishers.

Farr, James. "Political Theory." In *Experiencing Citizenship: Concepts and Models for Service-Learning in Political Science*. In Richard M. Battistoni and William E. Hudson, eds. Washington, DC: American Association for Higher Education.

Guarasci, Richard. 1997. "Community-Based Learning and Intercultural Citizenship." In *Democratic Education in an Age of Difference*, Richard Guarasci and Grant Cornwell, eds. San Francisco: Jossey-Bass.

Havel, Vaclav. 1997. "New Year's Address to the Nation." In *The Art of the Impossible: Politics as Morality in Practice*. New York: Alfred A. Knopf.

Hildreth, R.W. 2000. "Theorizing Citizenship and Evaluating Public Achievement," *PS: Political Science and Politics* 33 (September): 627-634.

Lappe, Frances Moore, and Paul Martin DuBois. 1994. *The Quickening of America: Rebuilding Our Nation, Remaking Our Lives*. San Francisco: Jossey-Bass.

Markus, Gregory, Jeffrey Howard, and David King. 1993. "Integrating Community Service and Classroom Instruction Enhances Learning: Results from an Experiment." *Educational Evaluation and Policy Analysis* 15 (Winter): 410-419.

Mendel-Reyes, Meta. 1997. "Teaching/Theorizing/Practicing Democracy: An Activist's Perspective on Service-Learning in Political Science." In *Experiencing Citizenship: Concepts and Models for Service-Learning in Political Science*, Richard M. Battistoni and William E. Hudson, eds. Washington, DC: American Association for Higher Education.

Morse, Suzanne. 1990. *Public Leadership Education: Skills for Democratic Citizenship*. Dayton, OH: The Kettering Foundation.

Morton, Keith. 1996. "Issues Related to Integrating Service-Learning into the Curriculum." In *Service-Learning in Higher Education: Concepts and Practices*, Barbara Jocoby, ed. San Francisco: Jossey-Bass.

Morton, Keith, and Richard Battistoni. 1995. "Service and Citizenship: Are They Connected?" *Wingspread Journal* 17 (Autumn):17-19.

National Association of Secretaries of State. 1999. *New Millennium Project – Phase I. A Nationwide Study of 15-24 Year Old Youth*: <http://www.nass.org/nass99.youth.htm>.

National Commission on Civic Renewal. 1998. *A Nation of Spectators: How Civic Disengagement Weakens America and What We Can Do About It*. College Park: Institute for Philosophy and Public Policy, University of Maryland.

Putnam, Robert D. 1993. *Making Democracy Work: Civic Traditions in Modern Italy* (with Robert Leonardi and Raffaella Y. Nanetti). Princeton: Princeton University Press.

Putnam, Robert D. 1995. "Bowling Alone: America's Declining Social Capital." *Journal of Democracy* 6 (January): 65-78.

Rimmerman, Craig. 1997. "Teaching American Politics through Service: Reflections on a Pedagogical Strategy." In *Education for Citizenship: Ideas and Innovations in Political Learning*, Grant Reeher and Joseph Cammarano, eds. New York: Rowman & Littlefield Publishers, Inc.

Rousseau, Jean-Jacques. [1772] 1972. *The Government of Poland*. Indianapolis: Bobbs-Merrill.

Saltmarsh, John, and Elizabeth Hollander. 1999. "Off the Playground of Higher Education." *PEGS Journal* 9 (Fall).

Sax, L.J., A.W. Astin, W.S. Korn, and K.M. Mahoney. 1999. "The American Freshman: National Norms for Fall 1999." Los Angeles, CA: Higher Education Research Institute.

Tocqueville, Alexis de. [1835] 1945. *Democracy in America*. New York: The Modern Library.

Wade, Rahima, ed. 1997. *Community Service Learning: A Guide to Including Service in the Public School Curriculum*. Albany, NY: SUNY Press.

Walker, Tobi. 2000. "The Service/Politics Split: Rethinking Service to Teach Political Engagement," *PS: Political Science and Politics*. 33 (September): 647-649.

Walt Whitman Center. 1996. *Measuring Citizenship: Assessing the Impact of Service Learning on America's Youth*. New Brunswick, NJ: Walt Whitman Center, Rutgers University.

Westheimer, Joel, and Joseph Kahne. 2000. "Service Learning Required." *Education Week*, January 26: <http://www.educationweek.org/ew/ew>.

# 4

# Service Learning and Civic Education in the Schools: What Does Recent Research Tell Us?

*Mary A. Hepburn*

*We are a nation founded upon active citizenship and participation in community life. We have always believed that individuals can and should serve. . . . Service, combined with learning, adds value to each and transforms both. Those who serve and those who are served are thus able to develop the informed judgment, imagination, and skills that lead to a greater capacity to contribute to the common good.*
*— Preamble to the Wingspread Report, Principles of Good Practice for Combining Service and Learning (Honnet and Poulsen 1989)*

The Wingspread Conference on service learning, cited above, helped to launch an era of high interest in utilizing community experiences to enhance citizenship education in American schools. Everywhere today educators hear and read the call for student service in the local community as a means to learning civic responsibility. Community service as part of schooling is advocated widely as more effective in civic education than relying solely on classroom instruction and textbooks.

Many teachers have reported lethargy and outspoken indifference by students when it comes to the study of government, public affairs, and civic life in traditional social studies courses. Recent national research supports these impressions. A study by the National Association of Secretaries of State (1999) reported that participating in public life, including voting, politics, and community activities, was rated very low in the interests of young Americans. Other studies (Mann 1999; Sax, Astin, Korn, & Mahoney 1998) provide evidence that young Americans are showing more interest in volunteering and service than in the 1980s, but their perspective has been individualistic and notably apolitical. Young people express an interest in helping others, but they generally have not viewed such activity as related to public needs and public political institutions.

The current student interest in volunteering may provide an educational means for young people to link civic and political life to volunteering and service. Advocates of service in education claim that when students find the linkage between courses in *school* and the needs and problems of the *community*, they will become more involved in both. Service learning offers a way of countering students' perceptions that there is no connection between "real life" and what they study in civics classes (Barber 1992; Hedin 1988; Task Force on Civic Education 1997).

What are the educational objectives that supporters of community service in schooling have in mind? Some proponents of student service in the community envision improved personal growth of students such as increased caring, altruism, and self-esteem, with good relationships between the school and the community as desirable by-products. However, for the political science, social science, and social studies teachers, who are the nation's civic educators in schools, community service learning has goals beyond motivating personal kindness in the society; service is viewed as a powerful means to boost knowledge of civic affairs and encourage greater participation. Service learning is advocated in social studies as a promising method by which young people will develop an awareness of civil society, civic identity, interest in the common good, and the beginnings of engagement in community life. Further, it is extolled as a practical instructional means to boost knowledge of civic affairs and civic skills and encourage greater participation (Battistoni 1997; Hedin 1988; Hepburn 1997; Kahne & Westheimer 1996; Kraft 1996; Shumer & Belbas 1996; Wade & Saxe 1996; Yates & Youniss 1996; Youniss, McLellan, & Yates 1997).

The theoretical basis of community service goes back to the writings of educational philosopher John Dewey (1916; 1938), who argued that school instruction should not be isolated from life experiences. Dewey's principle of *interaction* is to strengthen learning by bringing student inquisitiveness and the formal instruction that takes place in the classroom into interaction with the external environment of community activities. Such interaction can provide a training ground for civic education in democracy – involving the role of citizen groups in the community, the government, and public social and economic policy concerns. The idea is to move beyond just reading and talking about democracy to participating in it. A school curriculum that involves students in community work is considered to have the potential of increasing interest and insight into civic matters. Further, public service may be a vehicle for developing and honing skills of deliberation, communication, and participation related to community life (Barber 1992; Battistoni 1997; Hepburn 1997; Seigel & Rockwood 1993).

**What Types of Service Are in the Schools?**

Two terms are prominent in the literature about student service and volunteering: *community service* and *service learning*. How do they differ? *Community service* is broadly used to describe all types of service including individual and organized volunteer work that is not part of the school curriculum. Community service may be encouraged, arranged, and even required by the school, but it is not connected to school course work. *Service learning* is a particular form of community service that is curriculum-based. Service learning incorporates service in the community into school course work. The service experience is related to learning objectives in the curriculum, and it is connected to classroom studies by written activities and discussions.

How widespread is service learning in schools? Since the mid-1980s the numbers of school students participating in some type of community service is estimated to have increased about 36 percent (Shumer & Cook 1999). A recent survey by the National Center for Education Statistics (Skinner & Chapman 1999) found that 83 percent of high schools and 77 percent of middle schools in the United States had students participating in community service activities. But only 46 percent of high schools and 38 percent of middle schools had students in *service learning* programs. The National Service-Learning Clearinghouse reports that more than 6 million high school students and more than 5 million middle school students are participating in some type of community service. Only about half of these students, however, is actually involved in *service learning*. These data reveal that though student service activities are widespread, there have been far fewer students involved in the type of service that is part of an organized school course and combines in-school and out-of-school learning experiences. However, the numbers of students in curriculum-connected service are gradually increasing. Support from Learn and Serve America grants from the Corporation for National Service, along with assistance from state and private sources, has been guiding school programs away from unstructured community service toward curriculum-related service learning (Shumer and Cook 1999).

**Designing Service-Learning Programs: What Is Needed to Make Them Work?**

The last decade produced a large body of research on service learning programs in schools. It offers insights into the several attributes of effective service-learning programs that can assist educators in designing service courses to improve civic education. The research also provides an awareness of issues and problems that can arise. Among the features that have been found essential to a good service-learning program are (1) integration of student service into the content and activities of a school course; (2) planned periods of reflection on the service experience; (3) a long enough time in the service work; and (4) faculty, student, and community involvement in planning the program.

**Service Integrated into the Civics Curriculum**. Students gain more from service in the community when their service is carefully tied to a course or courses in the school curriculum and the service experience is clearly connected to the course content (Hedin, 1988; Raskoff & Sundeen 1998; Seigel & Rockwood 1993). Civic education service experiences, therefore, should be planned with well-thought-out learning objectives that fit the content of a course and unit of study and specifically address civic education. The service part of the course supplements and enriches the curriculum. Academic content and pedagogy – the readings, classroom lectures, and discussions – provide students with a knowledge framework that relates to their service. Then during and after service, students can interact by reviewing field experiences and relating them to classroom learning. The classroom experience, when related to service in the community, can build civic knowledge and develop students' skills in problem solving, communication, negotiation, and social action. Student service, however, is too often focused narrowly on improving the students' personal feelings of relevance and belonging in the community. If educators do not move instruction beyond personal development to an interest in participation and meeting the community's needs, then service is unlikely to contribute to civic responsibility, and students may fail to interpret that responsibility in terms of participatory citizenship (Niemi et al. 2000; Raskoff & Sundeen 1998; Rutter & Newman 1989).

Thus far, in only a few researched school programs have students learned civic participation as a means to influencing public policy, and few programs have resulted in students' gains in attitudes of political efficacy or inclinations toward citizen action (Boyte 1991; Conrad & Hedin 1991; Cowan 1997; Eyler & Giles 1997; Riedel 1999; Rutter & Newman 1989). While service learning has the potential for increasing students' intentions to be informed, to be active, and to vote, the educational procedure requires that the service assignment be related clearly to political processes. It must generate an awareness of the ways in which citizens can be involved in public policy decisions. Such service work might be in local government agencies, organized advocacy groups seeking environmental or political change, or the prevention of change in the locality. Zoning, land use, housing, and traffic issues offer high-interest learning experiences on how various groups in a local community can influence policies. The specific type of service makes a difference in how effectively learning objectives can be met. To build attitudes of political efficacy and civic involvement, the service and related curriculum content should include government, political issues, and/or social action (Hamilton & Zeldin 1987; Kim, Parks & Beckerman 1996; Yates & Youniss 1996). Teachers have to prepare students to develop skills of listening, application, interaction, and judgment on the service site. Back in the classroom, they can further deliberate and discuss the public context and community issues surrounding their observations and work experience. Thus they tie together the two worlds of learning. In the form of civic education, which integrates classroom and community experiences, teachers both teach *about* democracy and assist students in taking part in "the practice of democracy" (Seigel & Rockwood 1993, 69).

**The Importance of Reflection**. After evaluating eight school service programs more than a decade ago, and finding they had little effect on students' sense of civic responsibility, Rutter and Newmann (1989, 373) made a strong recommendation that future service-learning programs in civic education include reflective seminars focused on issues of "social responsibility," how to improve "the common good," and "opportunities for meaningful political participation." Numerous subsequent studies of service-learning programs in secondary schools have pointed to the great importance of planning and providing for students systematically to contemplate their service experience and its implications (Wade & Saxe 1996). For example, a study of a high school internship service-learning program that included teaching about local government and citizenship, participating in periods of reflection, using written journals about service-learning experiences, and participating in student seminars was found effective in generating learning gains (Hamilton & Zeldin 1987). A study of African-American high school juniors in a service-learning course found that reflective writing helped the students to think beyond their particular experience and to reflect on broader societal issues about social justice, poverty, health costs, racism, and housing (Yates & Youniss 1996). A study of both high school and middle school service learning compared the outcomes for students who had no reflective activities with those who did (Blyth, Saito & Berkas 1997). Over time, students in service who did *not* have reflective sessions expressed less responsibility toward civic involvement, toward the environment, and toward serving and helping others. They also found evidence that the students who had a systematic reflective experience in the classroom became more disengaged from school than the others.

The reflective component to service is usually structured into the course by requiring that students keep a journal about field experiences, take part in group discussions, and write short commentaries or term papers (Kraft 1996; Shumer & Belbas 1996). One review of reflective activities reported by teachers in ten service-learning programs found that the large majority (91%) of the teachers used group discussion, and a majority also used written reflection (72% papers, 62% journals) as well as applied projects (53%) (Blyth et al. 1997). Studies show that individual reflection and group discussion encourage students to think analytically and critically about their service and the issues associated with it. These teaching methods also give students opportunities to review what they have learned in the classroom in contrast to what they have seen and done in the community. Reflective activities prompt students to think, write, and talk about their observations, work, and concerns. But such contemplation and discourse usually does not "just happen" among the students. It has to be designed by educators into the total process of learning by students. The result of this reflective experience is provision of feedback about experiential activities that benefits students and informs teachers, school administrators, and community cooperators about the quality of service learning and civic education in their schools.

**Length of Service Time**. The duration of the service experience is significant. Very short periods of service appear to have little or no effect on students. Service that has a longer time period and averages more than an hour per day is more effective in achieving both personal and civic responsibility (Shumer & Belbas 1996). Students need enough time in the community to learn about the civic process involved and to form ideas about public problems and solutions. In a study of data from more than 4,000 students in grades 9-12, Niemi, Hepburn & Chapman (2000) found that short periods of service contributed little to learning. A minimum of 35 hours of regular sustained community service was associated with gains in students' political knowledge, participatory skills, and feelings of understanding politics. Studies of college students in service-learning courses have also indicated that programs of brief duration (such as service during holiday breaks) showed little or no effect. At least one or two semesters of regular service work in the community were needed to develop skills and attitudes needed for responsible and effective participation in civic and political life (Eyler & Giles 1997).

In a comparison of pre-tests and post-tests of secondary school service-learning programs, mostly in ninth-grade classes, students who participated more than 40 hours showed greater increases in attitudes of social responsibility and civic involvement than those who served for less time (Blyth et al. 1997). In another study, which was the final evaluation in a two-year study of the effectiveness of selected Learn and Serve America school-based programs, the impact on the students tended to fade in the year following the initiation of service participation, *except* for students who continued organized service. This longer term of service was related to positive effects on educational attitudes and school performance (Melchior 1998). Overall, the research indicates that when social studies/civic educators design a student service-learning course, the field activity should extend for at least a semester with approximately five or more hours per week so that students have at least 35-40 hours in the field. Even better would be a two-semester program with twice as many hours of service in the community.

**Faculty, Student, and Community Involvement**. Teacher preparation and planning is essential to a well-designed service-learning course. Indeed, studies have shown that most programs are initiated either by innovative teachers or administrators who have become interested in using the community for learning. Professional development opportunities provide some incentives for teachers. Grants and stipends are often available to initiate this teaching approach, and there frequently are opportunities to work with colleagues to study change and report the observations to other educators at professional meetings. In many cases, teachers who lead the service-learning program receive recognition from the community (Gulati-Partee & Finger 1996; Shumer & Balbas 1996). Teachers often decide to obtain or develop instructional materials that are applicable to the local community and appropriate for preparing their students for service, so advance time is needed by teachers to prepare for the integration of service into course work. For instance, a hands-on elections education program initiated in the St. Louis public schools reported that the first necessary steps for their service program were orientation and planning sessions for teachers (Kim et al. 1996).

Student interest and effort is central to the success of service learning. Students sense quickly that service in community agencies makes their role in learning about civic institutions and participation much more active than in traditional classes. If their service is long enough and allows for reflection on their experiences, then students are likely to see that their community activity is pivotal to the course. Students can be made partners in service projects if they are involved in the planning stages with teachers, administrators, and representatives of the community to determine how and where the community can be served and just how their particular assignment can contribute to the public good. And when students feel an "ownership" in the service program, they are more likely to pursue their work with pride and enthusiasm. Likewise, some responsibility in review and evaluation helps them understand how to make a difference in the community (Blyth et al. 1997; Gulati-Partee & Finger 1996; Schwartz 1987).

To assure that service learning is understood as more than volunteering and more than individual assistance and to emphasize its public contributions, the community agencies must be treated as partners in service programs. When service work is understood as a means to develop civic skills for living in a democracy, community leaders and community agencies/organizations must have a role in planning and final review. For example, evaluation of the Learn and Serve America programs (Melchior 1998) showed that community agencies overall expressed satisfaction with student workers; 90% of the agencies said that students had helped the agency improve their services to clients. Student participants had produced services that were valued at nearly four times the cost of the service-learning programs.

Students get into their service projects by taking part in initial preparations that begin in the classroom; however, it is in the community where students learn to work cooperatively with others and develop a civic conscience (Lisman 1998). Overall, service learning in schools benefits from cooperative planning and arrangements. Research shows that effective civic service is a two-way street (Blyth et al. 1997). Teacher and students must rely on support from school administrators and the public, and in turn school and community leaders need to receive feedback from students and teachers about the progress and exigencies of service programs.

## Making Sense of Service: Rationale, Case Examples, and Issues from Research

For civic educators who would organize and activate a program of service learning, it is essential to have a tested rationale, case examples that illuminate the process of civic education, and an awareness of key issues that can arise. Recent research offers all three.

**Rationale.** A study analyzing national data on political participation by voting-aged adults tested the relationship between political activity and political knowledge to determine if there is a connection between experiencing political activity and level of political knowledge (Junn 1991). The researcher found a reciprocal relationship supporting the theory that "participation and political knowledge feed on one another" (Junn 1991, 197). As people gain more knowledge of government and politics, they are more likely to participate; and when they participate politically, they gain more political knowledge. She concluded that "individuals gain cognitive skills or knowledge from their experience participating in the political system, and taking part in political activity enhances the level of knowledge individuals have of their government" (Junn 1991, 208). The reciprocal connection found in this study provides a strong incentive for high school programs that combine service in political institutions and organizations with courses in the civics curriculum. It suggests that students' service experiences in government and community politics will increase civic knowledge, and, in turn, will accelerate their inclination to participate.

The knowledge-service connection also receives support from results of the latest National Assessment of Educational Progress in Civics (Lutkus et al. 1999). Among the twelfth-grade students tested, 58% had done community service work during the past year. Twelfth-grade students who did volunteer work in their communities had significantly higher civic knowledge scores than those who had not (Lutkus et al. 1999, 101).

The rationale for community service in high school is given convincing support by a synthesis of several research inquiries into the effects of the participation of students in organized school-community activities conducted by Youniss, McLellan & Yates (1997). They analyzed five studies of the civic behavior of adults in relationship to their participation as youths in student government, community-based projects, 4-H, social service clubs, and other organizations during high school years. Adolescent involvement in the school community and the larger community had a bearing on later-life political interest and participation. The researchers found consistent evidence that participation in organized groups during high school contributes to the development of a civic identity that continues into adulthood and mediates civic engagement. Of particular interest to civic educators is a study by Verba, Schlozman, & Brady (1995) that found adult political participation to be strongly related to student involvement in high school government, clubs, and interest groups (excluding athletics). They found that high school can provide practical hands-on experiences, which train young people for civic participation as they learn forms of political discourse and consider differing points of view; and for those students who get this experience, it makes a difference in their adult lives. Community service that connects young people to the polity will help them gain civic identity. "Instead of thinking of society as determined by impersonal forces, youth recognize that their agency gives them responsibility for the way society is and for the well-being of its members" (Youniss et al. 1997, 625).

**Case Examples**. While broad-based studies linking active and abstract learning offer highly encouraging findings for development of service-learning programs, research on particular cases is also needed to provide insight into management of the experiential civic learning process. One example is found in the positive results of a study of a high school civics course with a local government internship program (Hamilton & Zeldin 1987). Using pre- and post-tests, the researchers compared the students in the internship program with a comparable student control group that did not have the experiential component in their studies. The internships in local government had two objectives: to teach about local government and to encourage interest and participation in civic affairs. Along with the service work, the internship course included some classroom instruction and interaction sessions between the students and local government policy makers. The students kept journals that were used in reflective activities, which the researchers observed were important to the learning process. At the conclusion of the semester, significant gains were found in the student interns' knowledge of local government. Using measures of *subjective political competence* and *perceived institutional responsiveness*, researchers also found positive changes in students' attitudes about their own capacities to influence political decisions as well as their perceptions of the likelihood that civic institutions would be responsive to citizens.

A more recent study (Riedel 1999) reveals that service learning in civic education is shaped by a school climate generated from faculty and administrator perceptions of service and its civic purposes. Riedel studied service-learning programs in six classes in four Minnesota high schools (3 public schools and 1 private school). He assessed the citizenship norms on which the programs were based and the effects of the service experience on participants' perceptions of citizen obligations. The researcher reported that the understandings of citizenship and the expectations for the service programs were different for each of the classes. Perceptions of the role of service learning in education appeared to fall on a broad continuum ranging from personal charity to activism in social-political change. Students in the private religious school class, who were encouraged to participate in seeking solutions to social and political problems, were more engaged in the political process. In one of the public school classes, citizen action was emphasized by the teacher, and these students were more engaged in the community politics related to their service. Educators leading the other four classes were more inclined to emphasize personal service rather than public commitment, which also made a difference in expectations. Riedel's work suggests to us that when planning service-learning programs for civic education, teachers and administrators should examine their understandings of the meaning of civic obligation and openly discuss the need to better educate students for active citizenship.

**Issues.** Among the issues raised by planning, observing, and evaluating school service learning are questions of the most effective grade level for beneficial community experience, the extent of outreach to students, and its cost effectiveness. Are experiential civics programs equally effective at both middle and high school levels? One study suggests not.

Research on selected school-based programs initiated under the auspices of Learn and Serve America evaluated service learning in seven middle schools and ten high schools across the country for the final report to the Corporation for National Service (Melchior 1998). The service-learning programs selected for review were "well designed" programs, all of which were integrated into the formal curriculum, had higher than average student service hours, regularly used written and oral reflection, and had been in operation for more than a year. One evaluation was conducted immediately after the student service course. It assessed "civic development" by measuring acceptance of cultural diversity, personal and social responsibility, and service leadership. Positive, significant impacts on high school students were found on all three civic development measures. Middle school students made significant gains on two measures of civic development – personal and social responsibility and service leadership. However, one year later, the follow-up evaluation showed that many of the immediate effects were gone, particularly among the middle school students. Exceptions to the decline were found in students who continued their involvement in organized community service beyond the initial course; their signs of civic development persisted. It should be noted that this research included some social studies classes but was not focused specifically on students in civics, government, or social studies courses. The final report, nonetheless, suggests that high school service-learning programs, whatever the subject matter, have a better chance of enduring effects than those in middle school, particularly if they involve students in longer-term service.

The extent of outreach to students from differing schools and backgrounds has been another question about service learning that is particularly apropos to education for civic responsibility. High school community service as a means to socializing young people to become civic participants becomes problematic if many are not included. A study which collected survey and interview data from the large number of both public and private high schools in Los Angeles County revealed that service learning had a selective reach among the students (Raskoff & Sundeen 1998, 75). Private religious schools (87%) were most likely to have community service programs, followed by public schools (81%), and private nonsectarian schools (77%). Taking into account the much larger population of the public schools, it was not surprising that the average *number of students* involved in the service programs was highest among the public schools. However, when the researchers examined the ratio of students in service learning compared to the total number of students in each school, the private schools were found to have the greatest proportion of students involved. The inverse relationship between the size of the student body and the proportion of students involved in service was attributed to (1) differing values in the private schools and (2) the logistical problems of providing and monitoring service opportunities in large public schools. The result is that only some students have service experience in their civic education.

Herein lies a key issue in service learning: to include all students should service learning be required? Advocates of mandatory service learning consider active service in the community as no different from other "required" courses that are considered basic to a high school education for all Americans (Barber 1991). Thus far, the National Center for Education Statistics (Kleiner & Chapman 1999) has determined that only 20 percent of students in grades 11 and 12 are in schools that both require and arrange community service. Another study (Raskoff & Sundeen 1998) found that a minority of both the public and private schools in Los Angeles County had mandatory service. However, based on their findings and a consideration of the resources and time needed to administer quality service learning, especially in large inner-city public schools, the researchers did not recommend mandatory programs for all schools. They estimate that if not all students are involved in community service courses, then it will be more manageable for the larger public schools and the school district to place student volunteers and effectively monitor their progress.

Civic educators must examine another question: if only one-half (or some other smaller portion) of the students participate in a service program that is well-focused on civic responsibility, what are the implications for the civic socialization of the students who are not involved? These several issues point up to the need to take into consideration the resources and commitments needed and the results that are sought when service learning is implemented to enhance civic learning in the schools.

## Conclusion

In an era when negativism toward government and politics and a poor understanding of political processes are contributing heavily to the civic disengagement of young Americans, there is a great need for more effective civic education practices in the school curriculum. Several types of research – surveys, controlled experiments, and analyses of cases – intimate that service learning designed with clear civic education objectives and a program well-integrated into the curriculum and community can make a difference. Service in the local community can connect learning to the prevailing student interest in volunteer work and add a lively, hands-on dimension to a school subject that has been in need of eye-opening and stirring reality.

Implementation of an adequate service-learning program is not an easy task for educators and school districts. Adequate professional preparation and educational resources are essential. Nevertheless, civic educators can be encouraged; most studies indicate that the results merit the effort.

Exposure to and involvement in the realities of local citizen concerns, public action, and government's response offer a rich and motivating context for civic learning. Thus, service-learning programs, connected solidly to the school curriculum and interactive pedagogy, may be able to peel away the political apathy and cynicism of students and lead to increased interest and awareness, healthy skepticism, and a greater degree of civic engagement. If so, it is worth the time, effort, and other costs necessary to create and sustain well-constructed service-learning programs.

## References

Barber, Benjamin R. 1992. *An Aristocracy of Everyone*. New York: Ballantine.

Barber, Benjamin R. 1991. "Mandate for Liberty: Requiring Education-Based Community Service." *The Responsive Community* 1 (Spring): 46-55.

Blyth, Dale A., Rebecca Saito, and Tom Berkas. 1997. "A Quantitative Study of the Impact of Service-Learning Programs." In *Service Learning: Applications from the Research*, Alan S. Waterman, eds. Mahwah, NJ: Lawrence Erlbaum.

Boyte, Harry C. 1991. "Community Service and Civic Education." *Phi Delta Kappan* 72 (June): 765-767.

Battistoni, Richard M. 1997. "Service Learning and Democratic Citizenship." *Theory Into Practice* 36 (Summer): 150-156.

Conrad, Dan, and Diane Hedin. 1991. "School-Based Community Service: What We Know from Research and Theory." *Phi Delta Kappan* 72 (June): 743-749.

Cowan, Jonathan. 1997. "The War Against Apathy: Four Lessons from the Front Lines of Youth Advocacy." *National Civic Review* 86 (Fall): 193-217.

Dewey, John. 1916. *Democracy and Education: An Introduction to the Philosophy of Education*. New York: Macmillan.

Dewey, John. 1938. *Experience and Education*. New York: Macmillan.

Eyler, Janet, and Dwight Giles Jr. 1997. "The Importance of Program Quality in Service Learning," in *Service Learning: Applications from the Research*, Alan S. Waterman, ed. Mahwah, NJ: Lawrence Erlbaum.

Gulati-Partee, Gita Finger, and William R. Finger. 1996. *Critical Issues in K-12 Service Learning: Case Studies and Reflections*. Raleigh, NC: National Society for Experiential Education.

Hamilton, Stephen, and Shepherd Zeldin. 1987. "Learning Civics in the Community." *Curriculum Inquiry* 17 (Winter): 497-200.

Hedin, Diane P. 1988. "The Power of Community Service." *Proceedings of the Academy of Political Science* 37 (2): 201-213.

Hepburn, Mary A. 1997. "Service Learning in Civic Education: A Concept with Long, Sturdy Roots." *Theory into Practice* 36 (Summer):136-142.

Honnet, Ellen P., and Susan J. Poulsen. 1989. *Wingspread Report: Principles of Good Practice for Combining Service and Learning.* Racine, WI: The Johnson Foundation.

Junn, Jane. 1991. "Participation and Political Knowledge." In *Political Participation and American Democracy,* W. Crotty, ed. Westport, CT: Greenwood Press.

Kahne, Joseph, and Joel Westheimer. 1996. "In the Service of What? The Politics of Service Learning." *Phi Delta Kappan* 77 (May): 593-599.

Kim, Simon, Sue Parks, and Marvin Beckerman. 1996. "Effects of Participatory Learning Programs in Middle and High School Civic Education." *The Social Studies* 87 (July/August): 171-176.

Kleiner, Brian, and Chris Chapman. 1999. *Youth Service-Learning and Community Service Among 6th Through 12th Grade Students in the United States: 1996 and 1999.* Washington, DC: National Center for Education Statistics.

Kraft, Richard J. 1996. "Service Learning: An Introduction to its Theory, Practice and Effects." *Education and Urban Society* 28 (February):131-159.

Lisman, C. David. 1998. *Toward A Civil Society: Civic Literacy and Service Learning.* Westport, CT: Bergin and Garvey.

Lutkus, Anthony et al. 1999. *NAEP 1998 Civics Report Card for the Nation.* Washington, DC: U.S. Department of Education.

Mann, Sheilah. 1999. "What the Survey of American College Freshmen Tells Us About Their Political Interest." *PS: Politics and Political Science* 32 (June): 263-268.

Melchior, Alan. 1998. *National Evaluation of Learn and Serve America School and Community-Based Programs: Final Report.* Waltham, MA: Brandeis University Center for Human Resources and Abt Associates, Inc.

National Association of Secretaries of State. 1999. *New Millennium Project: American Youth Attitudes on Politics, Citizenship, Government and Voting.* Lexington, KY: NASS.

Niemi, Richard G., Mary A. Hepburn, and Chris Chapman. 2000. "Community Service by High School Students: A Cure for Civics Ills?" *Political Behavior* 22 (March): 45-69.

Raskoff, Sally, and Richard A. Sundeen. 1998. "Youth Socialization and Civic Participation: The Role of Secondary Schools in Promoting Community Service in Southern California." *Nonprofit and Voluntary Sector Quarterly* 27 (March): 66-87.

Riedel, Eric. 1999. *The Effects of High School Community Service Programs on Adolescents' Civic Orientations.* Paper presented at the Annual Meeting of the American Political Science Association, September 2-5.

Rutter, Robert A., and Fred M. Newmann. 1989. "The Potential of Community Service to Enhance Civic Responsibility." *Social Education* 53 (October): 371-374.

Sax, Linda J., Alexander W. Astin, W.S. Korn, and K.M. Mahoney. 1998. *The Amer-*

*ican College Freshman: National Norms for All, 1998.* Los Angeles: Higher Education Research Institute, UCLA.

Seigel, Susan, and Virginia Rockwood. 1993. "Democratic Education, Student Empowerment, and Community Service: Theory and Practice." *Equity and Excellence in Education* 26 (September) 65-70.

Schwartz, Susan. 1987. "Encouraging Youth Community Service: The Broadening Role of High Schools and Colleges." *National Civic Review* 76 (July/August): 288-301.

Shumer, Robert, and Brad Belbas. 1996. "What We Know about Service Learning." *Education and Urban Society* 28 (February): 208-223.

Shumer, Robert, and Charles Cook. 1999. *The Status of Service Learning in the United States: Some Facts and Figures.* St. Paul, MN: National Service-Learning Clearinghouse at the University of Minnesota.

Skinner, Rebecca, and Chris Chapman. 1999. *Service Learning and Community Service in K-12 Public Schools.* Washington, DC: National Center for Education Statistics, US Department of Education, NCES 1999-0443.

Task Force on Civic Education. 1997. *PS: Political Science and Politics* 30 (December): 744- 745.

Verba, Sidney, Kay Lehman Schlozman, and Henry E. Brady. 1995. *Voice and Equality: Civic Voluntarism in American Politics.* Cambridge: Harvard University Press.

Wade, Rahima, and D.W. Saxe. 1996. "Community Service-Learning in the Social Studies: Historical Roots, Empirical Evidence, Critical Issues." *Theory and Research in Social Education* 24 (Fall): 332-359.

Yates, Miranda, and James Youniss. 1996. "A Development Perspective on Community Service in Adolescence." *Social Development* 5 (March): 85-111.

Youniss, James, Jeffrey A. McLellan, and Miranda Yates. 1997. "What We Know about Engendering Civic Identity." *American Behavioral Scientist* 40 (March/April): 620-631.

# 5

## Civic Education as a Craft, Not a Program

### *Harry C. Boyte*

*Citizenship is tackling problems and taking things into your own hands, not just sitting back and watching.*
*— Chou Yang, Sixth Grade, St. Bernard's School*

This chapter describes the roots, objectives, lessons, and effects of Public Achievement, a civic education initiative of the Center for Democracy and Citizenship that began in 1990. It is based on what we have called a "public work" approach to service learning (Boyte & Farr 1997). Public Achievement is now in seven communities and beginning in Northern Ireland. Over ten years, it has involved more than 10,000 young people, ages 8-18, and more than a thousand adult "coaches" in what we call public work projects designed, developed, and implemented by young people, with coaches' aid. These are usually undertaken over the course of a school year, and most are during the school day in participating schools, sometimes with supplemental integration into other curricular activities. Young people choose the issues they work on. Moreover, Public Achievement has involved young people in strikingly different cultural, income, racial, and economic backgrounds in public schools, Catholic schools, and different geographic locations. Thus, it furnishes a window into the civic interests of children and teenagers in our time. It has also proven a fertile ground for what can be conceived as a participatory action research project on citizenship and civic education (Greenwood & Levin 1998).

### Roots and Early History

*Public Achievement is a chance for kids to do something they love. We get into groups for different problems. We work together to solve the problems. The reason why I did Public Achievement is because things in the world are wrong. Public*

61

*Achievement and Dr. King are alike because we both made a difference in the world peacefully. We both look at the problems and solve them instead of blaming people.*
                                        *– Matt Anderson, 4th grade, St. Bernard's School*

Public Achievement has its roots in the civil rights (or "freedom") movement of the 1960s, especially in the Citizenship Education Program (CEP) of the Southern Christian Leadership Conference. CEP sponsored what were called citizenship schools – informal training and discussion groups organized in clubs, beauty parlors, church basements, and other settings. In these, one could witness often profound changes in outlook and identity among young people, sometimes children. Moreover, when black youth in the South, suffering the abuse of generations, developed courage and hopefulness about the possibility of change, they often transformed adult patterns of fatalism and hopelessness into activism and hopefulness.

The citizenship schools taught a philosophy of nonviolence and skills of citizen action. They were also infused with a deep, albeit critical, belief in the resources of American democracy; what Frederick Harris has called the combination of "ruly and unruly" civic commitments that characterized the African-American freedom tradition (Harris 1998).[1]

In Public Achievement these themes were translated into a set of criteria for the issues young people choose to take up. Issues must be (1) nonviolent, (2) legal, and (3) make a public contribution. The SCLC experience informed the framing of Public Achievement, which aims to develop active citizens for a flourishing democracy. Effort to theorize SCLC and populist movements also generated a political stance, which simultaneously emphasizes the distinctiveness of American democratic politics, as an alternative to socialist and labor politics, and stresses democracy as an unfinished work (Boyte 1989). In practical terms, this "civic populist" approach to civic education led to an interest in partnerships that confounded liberal-conservative lines, ranging from Catholic schools and ethnic groups to inner-city public schools.

Finally, Public Achievement embodies the concept of free spaces (Evans & Boyte 1986; 1992), and lessons of the most successful community organizing projects (Boyte 1989). From the treatment of free spaces, Public Achievement drew the importance of places in community and institutional contexts which youth "owned," where they could have wide latitude for experimentation, creation, and self-definition. From community organizing, it drew an original repertoire of core civic concepts and a stress on development of public talents and leadership, themes that seemed central elements in networks like the Industrial Areas Foundation. Core concepts included the idea of public life as a space for practical action on public tasks by diverse people. They included power and self-interest as relational and dynamic. In Public Achievement these ideas were frames with a notion of politics as a key dimension of the fabric of every environment, a framework called "citizen politics" (Boyte 1993).

Public Achievement was launched by the Humphrey Institute's Project Public Life (soon thereafter to be the Center for Democracy and Citizenship) in 1990 with a series of discussion groups among teenagers. Although conventional wisdom in the United States held that youth were apathetic and unconcerned, it soon became clear that young people – every group talked with – had deep concerns and problems they worried about. These ranged from violence, teen pregnancy, school relationships, and racial prejudice to the environment. Many expressed anger at school policies they felt were unfair, or at teaching approaches that failed to recognize their interests and intelligence. Youth in all the groups also said that adults had rarely asked their opinions on such issues – and almost never had imagined that young people could actually do anything about them. Other key themes of Public Achievement came out of this period, such as the concept of "coach" (young people liked the idea of adults as coaches more than any other role – advisor, teacher, mentor), and the usefulness of "public" (young people liked the idea of a public world, where they can interact with different kinds of people, far more than "community").

From its outset, Public Achievement stressed cooperative action. Its basis was teams coached by adults (usually young adults) who served as democracy guides. Young people chose projects around issues they were concerned with, and they developed strategies for action, usually over the course of a school year. The flagship school for Public Achievement was St. Bernard's, a K-8 elementary school in St. Paul, Minnesota, where the principal, Dennis Donovan, now the national organizer for Public Achievement, saw it as a way to teach students hope, courage, and skills of effective citizenship. He also wanted to change the way teachers taught and schools thought about education to include a central focus on young people's interests and concerns, and a large vision of schools as seedbeds of democracy. Donovan, St. Bernard's School, the Center for Democracy and Citizenship, and James Farr of the University of Minnesota created a strong partnership approach, which has continued to be the basic model for expansion of the project.

Early experience made visible the desire of young people for serious work on issues of importance to them. One group of seventh-grade girls, led by a girl who had previously been seen as having acute emotional disturbances and learning disabilities, developed a project that affected school culture on sexual harassment issues. In the course of the year's organizing, she personally underwent a striking change in her own behavior and motivation, becoming poised, confident, and academically successful. A group of third and fourth graders organized parents and neighborhood residents in a large peace march against violence. Fifth and sixth graders worked for four years to build a neighborhood playground, overcoming opposition from residents, gaining support from city officials and local businesses, and raising over $60,000. In his 1999 State of the State address, Minnesota Governor Jesse Ventura recognized the project.

### Lessons of Theory and Practice

Several lessons soon emerged. Initially, "coaches" had been recruited by signing up college students from a variety of classes, but the pattern lacked the level of accountability needed for in-depth, dependable work with teams. James Farr, who soon began to have all his students serve as coaches, offered a far better model. His coaches were from a single class that he took each week to the site. Moreover, they were learning political theory and civic concepts that they also used in their coaching. A second lesson soon became clear, moreover. Young people needed to be able to "map" the political cultures and traditions of the settings in which they were taking action and learn the interests and outlooks of others on different sides of their issues. Otherwise, they were liable to become simply angry protestors, unable to act with effectiveness. The usefulness of partnerships with community groups became apparent in two sites where such connections enhanced the depth and "seriousness" of the work: a partnership between Humboldt High School for Public Achievement and the Jane Addams School for Democracy, a community-based education and action center with Hmong and Latino residents, and St. Gregory's, a rural school in Maryville, Missouri. Joe Kunkle, a professor of political science at Mankato State University demonstrated the helpfulness of "master coaches," coaches who had coached before and serve as guides for first time coaches, in his work with Dakato Meadows Middle School. Sites like Holy Cross School in Kansas City, Missouri demonstrated the importance of what is called a "site coordinator," someone within the school setting whose job is to integrate Public Achievement into school cultures and curricula. From Eisenhower School in Kansas City, Kansas, the power of sustained use of the Public Achievement's civic language became clear in creating a counter "civic culture" in a school.

The guiding concept of Public Achievement came to be public work, meaning the visible effort of a mix of people to create some real outcome that makes a lasting difference in their community or the world. Public work proved a more powerful concept than "citizen politics" for youth to think with as they considered what contribution they would make. The public work concept also turned out to have rich, if not previously elaborately theorized, resonance in American political culture, with strong traditions in the Revolutionary Era, Civil War, settlement houses, land grant and other colleges, and New Deal work programs like the CCC and WPA (Boyte & Kari 1996).

## Civic Agency

*When I was first invited to participate in Public Achievement, what impressed me was that these students believed they had the power to change the world around them. At 22 years old I didn't think that I could do that. I heard stories of murals that had ended a school's graffiti problem, campaigns against chemical abuse, playgrounds being erected . . . Children without jobs, money, or influence proved that they could indeed have influence. Meanwhile, there I sat feeling powerless.*
    *– Joseph O'Shea, Coach, Hartford Middle School, Milwaukee*

The concept of public work, developed in Public Achievement (and other partnerships of the Center like the Jane Addams School for Democracy, Cooperative Extension, and colleagues concerned with recasting professional practice in public work terms) has proven a useful resource for theorizing civic agency. Recent scholarly publications (Putnam 2000) have reported widespread civic apathy among young Americans. Public Achievement suggests, in contrast, that such findings are functions of the relatively weak conceptions of civic agency that structure the questions. A more robust conception of civic agency illuminates the civic interests of a generation that, far from apathetic, is deeply worried about the public problems of our time and eager to have their energies enlisted in addressing them.

The Center's work has conceptualized different traditions and frameworks of citizenship: the idea of citizen as a voter, associated with liberal political theory, embodied in civic education approaches like civics; the idea of the citizen as volunteer, associated with communitarian theory and the modern service learning movement; and the concept of the citizen as civic producer or co-creator of a common world, what the Center for Democracy and Citizenship terms the public work or commonwealth framework (see Figure 5.1 at the end of this chapter). None of these models is wrong – indeed, discussing them is a way to highlight distinctive and different dimensions of citizenship. But the commonwealth approach emphasizes the powerful concept of the citizen as a "co-creator" of the common public world (Boyte & Kari 1996; Boyte & Farr 1997). It can be usefully linked to the sense of "society-making" that infused the citizenship schools of the civil rights movement. Then, it was evident that neither courts nor political leadership would desegregate the south. A large-scale process of "redefining citizenship" was necessary in order to tap the civic interests and energies of millions of ordinary African Americans and their allies. In our time, the concept of citizen as co-creator provides resources for an analogous project, advanced by the National Commission on Civic Renewal and others, to revitalize American democracy itself in a time of rapid change (National Commission on Civic Renewal 1998).

The evidence from Public Achievement indicates that this is a civically anxious generation, worried about problems that they feel no one is acting on, angry at the ways their talents are rarely enlisted. Their civic energy is evident in the statistics of involvement: often over 90% of kids choose to do Public Achievement, when coaching capabilities exist. Building on such experiences, Public Achievement's core theme is that young people are not simply citizens in preparation. They are citizens today. Reconceptualized civic agency creates a context for the reconceptualization of "politics." When Angela Mathews, a young leader in Public Achievement Northern Ireland, asked 100 PA members in the fall of 1999 whether they like politics, the majority (with no prompting or preparation) raised their hands. "It's because we are doing politics," Angela observed. "It's not simply something politicians do."

## Outcomes and Factors in Success

*Our kids generally come into Public Achievement feeling hopeless about the tremendous problems they see in their communities – drugs, crime, prostitution. Public Achievement unleashes hope in kids that they can actually take action to change things.*
*— Joe Groves, Teacher, Minneapolis*

Over the last two years, two teams of researchers have been undertaking an in-depth evaluation of Public Achievement participants, including team members, coaches, teachers, principals, and others in the environment. The Kauffman Foundation, a major funder of PA, has conducted extensive focus groups, survey research, and other forms of evaluation of public and Catholic schools implementing Public Achievement in the Kansas City region (Moore et al. 1998; Jianas et al. 1999). A second program evaluation coordinated by Nan Skelton, Associate Director of the Center, has been undertaken by Michael Baizerman, an internationally recognized authority on youth subcultures and evaluation, who is a professor at the University of Minnesota, and Robert Hildreth, a political theory graduate student, who has been a leader in coach training and materials preparation for several years. Their research involves qualitative interviews. It seeks to understand the "how" of Public Achievement's success (Hildreth 2000).

Public Achievement has often had a profound impact on children and young people involved. In the Kauffman evaluations, positive aggregate outcomes for youth include improved understanding of their issue, heightened sense of self-efficacy and self-confidence, mastery of public skills such as team work, public speaking, expressing opinions, respecting others' opinions, and increased ability to discuss and understand civic concepts. Public Achievement also affects coaches and often teachers and school cultures as well. For instance, coaches report much higher assessments of young people's public capacities and potential than before their experiences. In schools, 53% of teachers report significant changes in their own behavior as a result of Public Achievement, reflected in higher expectations for kids; talking more about public affairs; offering more experiential and service opportunities.

In the Skelton, Baizerman, and Hildreth evaluation, three elements of Public Achievement have emerged as especially significant to its impacts. They are (1) public achievement as a free space, (2) public achievement as a craft, and (3) public achievement as a site of democratic theorizing.

**Free Space**. From the beginning, Public Achievement has been conceived, in part, as a "free space," understood as a setting where young people have freedom to experiment, design their own work, and have a lively, open intellectual life. Young people choose to participate; they choose the issues on which to work; they create their own rules (one of the first acts of every team); they learn to hold each other accountable to the rules; they develop strategies and methods of their work, and, with the guidance of coaches, they do the work themselves, like making phone calls or writing letters or making public presentations.

Public Achievement is also a free space in offering a sharp contrast with the normal phenomenology of young people's lives. Young people live in a world of others' making, with rules, procedures, classes, structures that often seem pre-set, like granite mountains. Moreover, they are besieged by public problems that often seem intractable, from racial conflict and violence to teen suicide or teen pregnancy. Public Achievement breaks the omnipresent messages that reinforce fatalism – "nothing can be done about this"; or "you can't affect that, you're just a kid." Assessment indicates that the very invitation for young people to take action on such issues, with accompanying practical skills, strategies, methods, and coaching, often has a tremendous impact on young people's sense of the possible. The importance of Public Achievement as a space where normal roles and identities are partly transcended or bracketed has also become clear. Young people talk about Public Achievement repeatedly as a place of "freedom," where they can "let down their masks," and "be themselves."

**A Craft**. Public Achievement suggests that civic education and action are far better understood as democratic crafts than as programs.[2] The Public Achievement/public work approach as a democratic craft has three main elements.

Public Achievement decentralizes much decision making to the team level, while it also passes on knowledge in apprenticeship-type patterns. Although some measure of pre-training in approaches to group work are helpful, mainly Public Achievement is learning by doing. Coaches, in the best of cases, also have help and guidance from "master coaches," people who have coached well before.

Public Achievement stresses a process of reflection, evaluation, and development of intellectual skills and public talents, in ways that are not possible with program approaches or learning activities too tightly tied to preset curriculum. It creates multiple spaces for young people to take public leadership on public and community issues of concern to them. There are opportunities for young people to play diverse roles, and to develop many different talents such as public speaking, writing letters, working in a team, planning strategies, and mapping skills of many kinds, political and contextual, related to various political and social contexts.

Public Achievement is also craft-like in its stress on the expression of distinctive and particular public "signatures" or identities, not uniform or generic outcomes. It emphasizes team work of originality, creativity, and distinctiveness.

**A Site of Democratic Theorizing**. Public Achievement is a powerful "language world," with meanings that expand considerably beyond team projects and with multiple opportunities for young people to develop facility with concepts. As Hildreth has argued, "Using Public Achievement's conceptual and theoretical tools, teams build their own 'grounded theories' [which] opens spaces for thought, action and being within disciplinary discourses" (Hildreth 2000). Team members come to think more explicitly about themselves, the world, and their place in the world.

## Challenges

> *Everything our kids hear is 'What can I get?' Public Achievement teaches, 'What can I contribute? How can I shape the world around me?'*
> *– Jamie Suek, Teacher, Anderson Open School, Minneapolis*

There are challenges to sustaining and expanding Public Achievement. Concepts such as the citizen as co-creator, or power as relational and interactive, or public life as an arena of difference and practical work with others on significant tasks – these are powerful tools for civic education

and citizenship. But they also go against the normal structures and practices of a highly commercial and technicized society. Few spaces or experiences exist that prepare people to think broadly about the "why" of their
efforts.

Public Achievement is developing expansion strategies based on a
"craft culture" approach. Its ultimate future is also linked to larger civic
ferment. Some, like the National Commission on Civic Renewal, have
seen stirrings of a broad citizen movement. Campus Compact discerns
signs of a "democracy movement" in higher education (Ehrlich 1999).

If we are at the threshold of a broad movement for democratic revital-
ization, young people again will play critical and energizing roles. In this
process, civic education will need to deepen and spread as a robust craft,
not simply a skill set or instruction in civic information or education about
relatively static roles. Public Achievement will furnish resources to make
a difference in how civic education is done, and what it can achieve.

## Figure 5.1

## Models of Democracy, Citizenship, and Civic Education*

|  | Civics | Communitarian | Commonwealth |
|---|---|---|---|
| What is democracy? | Representative institutions, the rule of law | Representative government and civil society | Work of the people, creating public things (including public institutions) |
| What is politics? | Distribution of goods, services (who gets what, how, when) | Generating a spirit of community | Creating the "commons" |
| Citizenship | Voter | Volunteer | Co-creator |
| Professional role | Intervening with expert knowledge | Facilitating, building consensus | Catalyzing people's energy and cultivating people's talents for public work |
| Government role | "For the people": to provide services, guarantee rights | "Of the people": to express and promote civic values | "By the people": to catalyze public work; provide tools for public work |
| Civic Education | Programs that teach about laws, elections, separation of powers, etc., e.g., Close-Up | Programs teaching values and civic responsibility, e.g., most community service, service-learning programs | Projects teaching skills, practices, habits, and values of working with others on public tasks, and reworking institutions, e.g., Public Achievement |

*This table describes three approaches to citizenship and civic education based on three ways democracy and citizenship are understood: (1) The "civics" approach conveys knowledge about government (e.g., how a bill becomes law; separation of powers; elections) and citizens are mainly "private citizens," with rights and a few responsibilities like voting and paying taxes; (2) the "communitarian" approach sees the model citizen as a caring volunteer; citizens are responsible members of a community, and a citizenship education focuses on teaching habits of voluntary involvement; and (3) the "commonwealth" approach rests on citizens as co-creators of a common world, doing the work of democracy, not only at elections but "every day." Here, civic education involves multiple opportunities for students to do public work with others and develop traits of boldness, political skill, courage, and effectiveness in shaping and changing the world.

## Notes

1. I worked in SCLS's Citizenship Education Program as a Field Secretary as a teenager in 1965-65, and often witnessed transformations in sense of self, confidence, and agency.

2. The theme of "craft" is my own interpretation of Hildreth's conclusions, which stress "work [that] takes place in the 'real world' with weighty consequences," though Baizerman and Hildreth agree craft is a useful term. The Center for Democracy and Citizenship has come increasingly to find the concept of "craft" and "public craft" of use, because it highlights traditions of practical wisdom and integrates these with a theoretical perspective on knowledge-making in the pragmatist vein. See, for instance, my essay, "Professions as Public Crafts," prepared for the Wingspread Conference on the New Information Commons, January 2000, and also Scott Peters' treatment of earlier traditions in cooperative extension, "Mission Drift or Renewal? Recovering an Historical Grounding for Assessing Cooperative Extension's Civic Work." Both are available on the public work web site, under new information commons and civic mission, respectively, Our colleague William Doherty of the University of Minnesota, has undertaken several linked pilot efforts under the rubric of "families and democracy" to develop a public work "craft" approach to family professional practice. He described his experiences, lessons, and successes in "Family Science and Family Citizenship: Toward a Model of Community Partnership with Families," the Presidential Address to the National Council on Family Relations, November 1999, to be published this year.

## References

Boyte, Harry C. 1989. *Commonwealth: A Return to Citizen Politics*. New York: Free Press.

Boyte, Harry C. 1993. "Civic Education as Public Leadership Development." *PS: Political Science and Politics*, 26 (December): 763-769.

Boyte, Harry C., and Nancy N. Kari. 1996. *Building America: The Democratic Promise of Public Work*. Philadelphia: Temple University Press.

Boyte, Harry C., and James Farr. 1997. "The Work of Citizenship and the Problem of Service-Learning." In *Experiencing Citizenship: Concepts and Models for Service-Learning in Political Science*, Richard M. Battistoni and William E. Hudson, eds. Washington, DC: American Association of Higher Education.

Ehrlich, Thomas, et al. 1999. *Presidents' July 4th Declaration on the Civic Responsibilities of Higher Education*. Providence: Campus Compact.

Evans, Sara M., and Harry C. Boyte. 1992. *Free Spaces: The Sources of Democratic Change in America*. Chicago: University of Chicago Press.

Greenwood, Davydd J., and Morten Levin. 1998. *Introduction to Action Research*. London: Sage Publications.

Harris, Frederick. 1998. "Will the Circle be Unbroken? The Erosion and Transformation of African American Civic Life." *Report from the Institute for Philosophy and Public Policy*. College Park: University of Maryland.

Hildreth, Robert W. 2000. "Theorizing Citizenship and Evaluating Public Achievement," *PS: Political Science and Politics*. 33 (September): 627-634.

Jianas, Linda, Tricia Hellmer, and Robin Jones. 1999. *Public Achievement–Citizenship in the Heartland: Year Two Evaluation*. Kansas City: Ewing Marion Kauffmann Foundation.

Moore, William P., Linda Jianas, Tricia Hellmer, Robin Jones, and Stephanie Gonzalez. 1998. *Public Achievement in Kansas City: Evaluation of the First Year of Implementation*. Kansas City: Ewing Marion Kauffmann Foundation.

National Commission on Civic Renewal. 1998. *A Nation of Spectators: How Civic Disengagement Weakens America and What We Can Do About It*. College Park: Institute for Philosophy and Public Policy, University of Maryland.

Putnam, Robert D. 2000. *Bowling Alone: The Collapse and Revival of American Community*. New York: Simon & Schuster.

# 6

# Effects of Public Deliberation on High School Students: Bridging the Disconnection Between Young People and Public Life

*Iara Peng*

As people think about the problems of our democracy, they most frequently mention a host of challenges, such as government corruption, the integrity of public officials, or the corrosive influence of money on politics. But a discussion around these kind of issues without mention of what Harry Boyte and Nancy Kari (1996) call the "real crisis" of democracy – the disengagement of ordinary people from productive involvement in public affairs – leaves the conversation incomplete. The national concern about the steady decrease in the engagement of citizens in public life, along with efforts to bridge the disconnection between citizens and public life, have propelled the question of how to best educate young people for engagement in public and political life to the forefront of the citizenship education agenda.

Citizens' civic capacities and responsibilities are not limited to voting or keeping up on current affairs. As Thomas Jefferson said, "Every man is a participator in the government of affairs, not merely at an election one day in the year but every day" (Ford 1903, 278). Similarly, David Mathews, president of the Kettering Foundation, observed: "A citizen is someone active in the public life of his community and country. Citizens are more than individuals living responsible private lives" (1995, 274). If we accept this view of democratic citizenship, which requires people to engage in public life, then we must further explore how citizens can best develop the necessary knowledge, skills, and habits to become active participants in democratic public life.

## Education for Democratic Citizenship

The preparation of young people for citizenship has traditionally focused on providing a basic understanding of how our government works – the three branches of government or how a bill becomes a law. A more complete education for democratic citizenship might help students not only gain a basic understanding of the structure and mechanics of our democratic government and their underlying principles, but also to learn what it means to be a citizen engaged in the democracy of everyday life. John J. Patrick, for example, argues that effective education for democratic citizenship satisfactorily treats four basic components: (1) knowledge of citizenship and government in democracy, (2) cognitive skills of democratic citizenship, (3) participatory skills of democratic citizenship, and (4) virtues and dispositions of democratic citizenship (1999, 34; see also Figure 1.1 in Chapter 1).

Several promising efforts aim to equip students with more powerful components of knowledge, skills, and habits of democratic citizenship to be active participants in their communities. Service learning, for example, provides students with opportunities to develop civic skills and virtues by connecting academic classroom-based instruction with out-of-school community projects and activities. Public Achievement, a national youth initiative of the Center for Democracy and Citizenship at the Humphrey Institute of Public Affairs, involves young people in what Boyte and Kari (1996) call "public work" – the ongoing effort of working with a diverse group of people to make a lasting contribution and solve public problems.

Classroom-based strategies that emphasize civic efficacy and public responsibility by teaching young people the skills of public deliberation represent a third approach to education for democratic citizenship. This chapter describes the results of a pilot study to assess the enduring effects of public deliberation on students, who learn about and participate in National Issues Forums (NIF). Their teachers incorporate NIF in the classrooms to equip students for active citizenship.

NIF, an informal, nonpartisan network of civic and educational organizations, convenes forums for public deliberation in hundreds of communities across the nation. NIF is rooted in the notion that citizens need to come together to deliberate about common problems in order to begin making the hard choices required to address them. Over the past 18 years, hundreds of community groups – including civic, service, and religious organizations, as well as libraries, high schools, community colleges, and universities – have encouraged public deliberation by holding NIF forums.[1] Forums, which are typically 90-minutes to two-hours long, bring citizens together to "work through" complex public issues, weigh costs and consequences associated with different choices or approaches to public policy, and make judgments about the range of actions that they, as a public, can support.[2] David Mathews and Noelle McAfee described public deliberation this way:

> Public deliberation is one name for the way people go about deciding how to act. In weighing – together – the costs and consequences of various approaches to solving problems, people become aware of the differences in the way others see those costs and consequences. That enables them to find courses of action that are consistent with what is valuable to the community as a whole. In that way, the public can define the public's interests – issue by issue.(Mathews & McAfee 1999, 1)

## NIF and Public Deliberation in the Classroom

Arguably, high school teachers who use NIF in their classrooms are contributing to the creation of a deliberative culture through which students can make politics their own. The idea of teaching deliberative democracy, as exemplified through NIF, assumes that people are capable of becoming public actors who can deliberate together, make sound choices, and take responsibility for their communities and the nation. Thus, education for citizenship in a deliberative democracy emphasizes preparing young people to understand the complexity of issues, recognize and assess trade offs, make informed choices about how to deal with a public issue, and work together as members of a public. One educator who uses NIF in her classroom describes the forums as "the closest thing to real citizen activity. In fact it *is* citizen activity. It's not fabricated or contrived. It is education linked to the real world, so it's the best form of civic learning" (Mathews 1996, 282).

Assessing the impact of citizenship education efforts is exceedingly difficult (Mathews & McAfee 1999, 2). For example, while some research suggests that learning public deliberation may help young people become more involved and may lead to new civic initiatives,[3] the deeper significance of deliberation, which is not captured by the creation of new programs, is still relatively unknown. As Jane Mansbridge (1995, 1) says, "Participation in democratic decisions makes participants better citizens. I believe this claim because it fits my experience. But I cannot prove it."

A recent pilot study, "The Enduring Effects of National Issues Forums (NIF) on High School Students," conducted by Doble Research Associates, a non-partisan public interest research firm based in Englewood Cliffs, New Jersey, provides insight into how young people are affected by their exposure to public deliberation and participation in NIF.[4] Doble Research partnered with four teachers who use NIF in their classrooms to teach deliberation, a more robust concept of politics, and the essential roles of a citizen in public life.[5] The goal of the study was to identify the enduring effects on high school students of learning about and participating in NIF in the classroom (Doble Research Associates 1999).

For citizens to be engaged and responsible, certain skills such as identifying appropriate issues for public deliberation, naming and framing them, and being able to deliberate are critical. Though the pilot study shed some insight into how public deliberation through NIF equips students with certain knowledge and habits, the study found the strongest indications of substantial change in the set of *skills* for citizenship that young people cultivated. And so, this chapter focuses on the skills of citizenship that high school students developed as they learned and experienced public deliberation through NIF.

To explore the extent to which the students acquired knowledge, habits, and skills of democratic citizenship, Doble Research interviewed 49 high school students, who had learned about public deliberation in a series of five three-hour-long focus groups. See Figure 6.1 at the end of this chapter.

The groups were conducted as follows: the students first discussed their courses in which NIF was used to teach deliberative democracy, how the material was presented, and their experiences with deliberation. Students also shared information about their out-of-class participation in the community and some general thoughts about what makes a good citizen. Each group was then presented with three scenarios for the students to address together. Each scenario was designed to be complex and challenging for the students, so as to learn whether, and to what degree, students would freely draw on what they had learned in their NIF courses.

The first scenario involved a fatal shooting in a high school.[6] The moderator read aloud this background to the students:

> A high school in a medium-size community has an ethnically diverse student body. One day, a black student is shot by a fellow student who is Hispanic. The media reports that it is a gang-related shooting though students at the high school say it was not. But tensions at the school are running high. Some community leaders see this as the latest in a series of incidents in a tense, ethnically divided community, and they are concerned that things may flame up out of control.

The students were informed that since they had experience with NIF, the principal and community leaders wanted them to review an NIF issue book, *Growing Up at Risk*,[7] and make a recommendation about what, if anything, the school could do using that book to ease tensions in the high school. Specifically the moderator asked the students to give advice about how a forum on this issue should be organized and structured. The exercise was designed to learn how the students would address a difficult community problem.

In the second scenario, the moderator began by reading aloud the following background information to the students:

> The community faces an impending crisis regarding the disposal of solid waste. To date, its solid waste – its garbage and trash, including newspapers – has been put into a landfill, which is filling up. There are four ways on the table of dealing with solid waste: source reduction, recycling, a new landfill, or incineration, each of which has costs or trade offs.

As part of the exercise, the students were told that scientists did not agree about the safety of incinerators. Though most scientists thought that a properly run incinerator is safe, the moderator said that a minority considered them unsafe, and a fair number were not sure which view was correct. The exercise was designed to explore whether the students could deliberate and move toward a reasoned judgment about a particularly complex issue where there was considerable uncertainty among experts. The students were then asked to participate in a forum that might serve as the model for a community-wide forum on the issue.

In the third and final scenario, students were asked what their school should do about a pressing issue not yet framed for deliberation – how students dress at school. The exercise was designed to see if, given the opportunity, the students would name and frame an issue for public deliberation, then consider the costs and consequences together in a deliberative atmosphere.[8] The moderator gave the students the following background information to begin the final part of the focus groups:

> The local high school is considering whether to require all students to wear school uniforms: a tan shirt and green tie for boys, and a green jumper and tan blouse for the girls. Supporters of the idea are concerned that some boys are wearing their pants low on their hips while some girls are dressing provocatively, which, taken together, make it more difficult to maintain an atmosphere conducive to learning in the school. Others are concerned about the financial burden that would be placed on students' families who would have to purchase the uniforms.

The students were asked how they would address the issue and how the school should approach it. After framing the issue, the students were asked to conduct a forum that might serve as the model for a community-wide forum on the issue.

## The Effects of Deliberation on High School Students

This pilot study provided new insights into how public deliberation, as exemplified in NIF, contributes to students developing certain knowledge, habits, and skills of democratic citizenship and gaining a better understanding of their role as members of the public in a democratic civil society. As noted above, components of education for democratic citizenship include knowledge of citizenship and government in democracy. Students should master basic knowledge about, for example, "ongoing tensions that raise public issues," and "practices of democratic citizenship and the roles of citizens" (Patrick 1999, 34). The Doble study found that students strongly demonstrated command over certain concepts, including that the public has the capacity to deal with a complex issue as long as it is presented, or framed, in public terms, and that making a decision about any public issue inevitably means making trade-offs.

In addition to demonstrating increased civic knowledge about how to approach a complex issue, the students we interviewed conveyed command over something more: they were confident when presented with a difficult issue, imaginative when digging into possible options, reflective when considering consequences, and invested in the decisions they made. They seemed to have gained new insights about what it means to be a citizen. Rather than settling into bystander roles, many were eager to get involved in community life and had clear ideas about how to do so. Since attitudes are usually developed gradually, over time, assessing the impact of teaching for attitude development is difficult; nevertheless, the students' comments suggest that NIF had a deep impact on how they engage with issues and interact with others outside the classroom in a public context.

Becoming an "actor" in public life involves more than just acquiring knowledge and ideas; it also means *practicing* citizenship. To be prepared for active roles in public life, students must have opportunities to develop skills in, for example, making decisions about public issues or thinking critically about public life. Given the right opportunities, students can learn to integrate skills that reflect what they learn into their daily lives, thereby building a sense of agency about public issues and community life. Their experiences with NIF and deliberative democracy gave many students a desire to embrace the responsibilities of citizenship. As one State College student said, "I learned [through my NIF course] how to get involved in the community [and how to] talk with strangers about our [common] problems. [I learned how] to be an [active] citizen."

In the study, Doble Research found that to a considerable extent, the students demonstrated command over eight skills of citizenship in a deliberative democracy.

**1. Listening carefully to others.** Making decisions together in a democracy involves the ability to listen to and understand other people and points of view, even if these viewpoints are ultimately not agreeable. Through their exposure to NIF, many of the students clearly developed this skill. A young man from Peterborough said that in a forum, "You get to listen to all sides and [then] develop an intelligent opinion about the issue." A young man from Dothan said:

Usually people don't get to hear other people's opinions on an issue because they're too busy trying to express their own. In a forum, we listen to each other and let each person express their point of view. We learn to control ourselves and listen more.

**2. Developing a public way to talk about problems.** The NIF motto is: "A different way to talk, another way to act." One central idea behind NIF is that most issues are *public* or *common* concerns and, as such, require a public to deliberate thoughtfully about them. A student from Dothan implied that he understood this concept when he said that because of his experience with NIF, "We now know that when you have a problem, it helps to get a group together to discuss it." A young woman from Keyser made a similar point, saying, "In order for us to make a decision [about school violence], we need to deliberate [collectively]."

**3. Naming and framing an issue for public deliberation.** Only when a problem is named in "public terms," terms the non-expert citizen can understand, can public deliberation take place. The way an issue is named and framed can predetermine the public's sense of ownership about, and connection to, the issue. NIF presupposes that people are best able to participate in a democratic society if they deliberate and make decisions about issues that are named and framed in public terms. This enables people to access and understand issues, and consider them objectively and realistically, in light of their costs and consequences.

Students realized the importance of the way an issue is named and framed, and most students developed the ability to name and frame an issue for public deliberation. A young woman from Keyser said that with regard to school shooting:

We need to create a good framework [for public deliberation] . . . come up with choices . . . like how to help little kids, figure out ways to make the school safer, and make sure students don't go crazy and shoot people.

One of the most striking results of this study was the students' rejection of the framework presented to them about the shooting incident. Recall that in this scenario the students were asked to imagine that, because of their NIF experience, the principal wanted their recommendation about what, if anything, could be done to ease tensions in the high school and in the community. We expected the students to immediately recommend convening a forum; but in four of the five groups, students rejected the framework, saying that it did not speak to some important aspects of the issue or reflect what many people considered valuable. The students thought the initial framework precluded public deliberation since not all voices were represented. And so, they insisted on reframing the issue to include other voices and to identify other ways of approaching the problem. This is a strong indication that the students deeply understood the concept of publicly naming and framing an issue for public deliberation.

**4. Engaging with, understanding, and getting a handle on complex issues.** Public deliberation as practiced in NIF exemplifies a well-known quotation from Thomas Jefferson:

> I know no safe depository of the ultimate powers of the society but the people themselves; and if we think them not enlightened enough to exercise their control with a wholesome discretion, the remedy is not to take it from them, but to inform their discretion by education.[9]

Students' comments indicated that they had the capacity to understand, deliberate, and reach informed judgments about even the most complex issues. As you may recall, the students were asked about solid waste disposal, an issue with several areas of expert uncertainty.[10] The students adeptly engaged in a deliberation around this complex issue, without being paralyzed by the areas of expert uncertainty. A young woman from Keyser implied that the issue of solid waste disposal has many facets, and, as such, is not simple to address. She said, "Dealing with the trash problem by recycling Styrofoam is just taking care of one [part of the] problem. You can't stop there [because] there are other parts [to the problem] that we also need to think about."

**5. Using deliberation to make decisions.** In their forums, many students learned to deliberate about public issues, to weigh together the costs and consequences, and to try to find courses of action consistent with what was valuable to their group as a whole. In the process, they developed new decision-making skills rooted in the concept of public deliberation. A young woman from Peterborough described the difference between deliberation and debate, saying, "In a deliberation, you get to hear everyone's ideas, whereas in a debate, it seems like the only purpose is to say, 'I'm right.'" A young woman from State College said:

> It's really important [before having the first forum] to discuss the differences between debating and deliberating. Deliberation is a much more powerful tool [than debate].

**6. Including the voices of people who are not in the room before taking action.** NIF encourages forum participants to weigh diverse points of view before deciding on a course of action, including the views of those who are not in the room. Students demonstrated an understanding of the importance of including and weighing the voices of people who may not be in the room before deciding on a course of action. Speaking about the solid waste issue, a young woman from Dothan implied that much could be gained by imagining what others might say:

> If we're considering reducing the amount of [solid] waste [by] using cloth diapers, we need to find out what people with babies think. Wouldn't it be an inconvenience for them?

**7. Identifying the general, common, or public interest.** Students' comments suggested that they were able to consider what was valuable to the group in terms of the common lives of its members, or what might sometimes be thought of as the general, common, or public interest. For example, when asked which option he would choose to effectively deal with the school dress issue, a young man from Peterborough said:

> For myself, I'd say [we should require] school uniforms. But for the school [as a whole, taking into consideration the views of other students], I'd say [we should adopt] the dress code.

**8. Reaching a reasonable, considered judgment about how to deal with an issue.** Through NIF, students also learned how to reach a reasonable judgment about an issue. This ability is, of course, related to other skills of democratic citizenship, especially weighing costs and consequences and hearing diverse viewpoints. To illustrate the idea of what a "reasonable judgment" involves, consider this comment about the shooting incident from a young Keyser woman:

> [Working to address the problem of school violence] could take a long time; changes won't happen overnight . . . You can't set a time limit on when you have to solve a problem, especially since there may be more tension on different subjects than others.

## Conclusion

Many educators have reached the view that traditional high school civics classes do not effectively equip students to be involved actively in their communities, or to understand their roles as citizens in a democratic civil society. This research has found that teaching public deliberation, as exemplified in NIF, not only helps students gain new knowledge about citizenship, it helps them develop citizenship skills and see how to integrate them into daily life. When asked what students learn through NIF, one of the teachers who worked on this project said:

They are learning valuable skills about listening and communicating – and are linking these skills to citizenship. They use NIF as a piece of an overall picture of what is required of an American citizen for our democracy to function.

In order to become active, public citizens in a democratic society, young people need to acquire fundamental knowledge, develop skills, and internalize certain virtues and dispositions of democratic citizenship. These basics are not related to ideology or particular points of view. Rather, they are the foundation upon which young people develop their perceptions about their role in democratic political and civic life. Cynicism and disconnectedness – perhaps the two greatest threats to democratic society – are best thwarted when young people are equipped with a strong foundation that enables them to take active, effective, and responsible roles in public life.[11]

**Figure 6.1**

| Students | High School | City/State | NIF Experience |
|---|---|---|---|
| Thirteen seniors | Northview High School | Dothan, AL | Seniors in a U.S. Government course deliberated together using a locally framed issue book, "Governing Alabama." As they participated in forums, students focused on learning how to determine whether deliberation was happening. |
| Twelve ninth-graders | Keyser High School | Keyser, WV | NIF was used in these ninth graders' World History course as a way to teach about deliberation and to connect the study of history to each student's daily life. |
| Six ninth-graders | Contoocook Valley Regional High School | Peterborough, NH | The use of NIF began as a result of a community-wide educational initiative organized by community members who read David Mathews' *Is There a Public for Public Schools?* As part of a larger program, the Civic Action Project, first-year students in an American Citizenship I course participated in three in-class forums. |
| Six seniors | Contoocook Valley Regional High School | Peterborough, NH | Seniors, in an independent study elective, participated in study circles and NIF forums in the community. Students helped convene eight community-wide forums and some students moderated the forums. |
| Twelve seniors | State College Area High School | State College, PA | In their current issues class, seniors focused on deliberative democracy through NIF and other resources, including David Mathews, "Making Choices Together: The Power of Public Deliberation," and materials from American Promise and the Study Circles Resource Center. |

## Notes

1. Public Agenda, working in collaboration with The Kettering Foundation, prepares new issue books each year designed to stimulate public deliberation on issues common to people across the country. The subjects are decided by polling the citizens in the NIF network. These are called National Issues Forum issue books. An NIF issue book contains at least three basic choices about how to view each issue. Then it reviews the reasons those who share that perspective have for their views and the concerns others have about them. Each choice is discussed in terms of the strategic facts that make it important, but also in terms of the things held valuable by those who support it. This careful, nonpartisan way of presenting each choice allows citizens to weigh carefully decisions that are necessary to address the issue. For more information see David Mathews and Noelle McAfee, *Making Choices Together: The Power of Public Deliberation* (Dayton, Ohio: The Kettering Foundation Press, 1999).

2. Moderators encourage participants of all ages to weigh carefully a variety of approaches to dealing with the problem, not just one or two specific solutions. The goal is to create some common ground for action, some sense of direction, and an appreciation for the interdependence of different purposes so people can act together.

3. One example of an effect of deliberation is from a series of public forums held across Birmingham, Alabama on the issue of "Kids at Risk." One direction forum participants settled on led to a program called CARES or Comprehensive at Risk Educational Services, run by young people at eight high schools. Three hundred and fifty young people now serve on advisory councils and conduct weekly meetings. Other programs that grew out of the forums include a teen employment program and Camp Birmingham, a youth-run camp for low-income youngsters. See Mathews and McAfee, *Making Choices Together*, p. 2.

4. To order a copy of this study visit <www.kettering.org>.

5. It is important to note that previous research by the Kettering Foundation and the Harwood Group shows that some teachers see NIF as pedagogy, not politics. Some teachers are using NIF materials to teach about a complex issue, such as social security, rather than to teach about a different concept of politics and the role of a citizen in public life. See Michael Perry, "Teachers' Project: Observations from Interviews in a Focus Group," The Harwood Group, 1992 and Kristin Cruset, "Deliberation in the Classroom," report to the Kettering Foundation, 1998. The four teachers who partnered with us were David Dillon from State College Area High School, State College, Pennsylvania; Jon Hal, Contoocook Valley Regional High School, Peterborough, New Hampshire; Peggy Hanahan, Northview High School, Dothan, Alabama; and Jennie Shaffer, Keyser High School, Keyser, West Virginia. The teachers agreed to review the research design, describe at length how they use NIF in their courses, recruit students for the focus groups, make all

the arrangements for the sessions, attend the focus groups as participant-observers, and debrief after the session and again by telephone sometime later.

6. The scenario was based on an incident in Panama City, Florida. In the aftermath of the shooting, a forum was held that was broadcast locally and fed to 2000 students at the high school. An abridged version of the issue book, "Growing Up at Risk" was used as a handout for students in the focus groups. They were presented with four choices for approaching the issue: teach values; restore order; provide care; build futures. For a copy of the issue book, visit <www.nifi.org>.

7. The framework on the issue of solid waste was developed for a 1990 study by Public Agenda for the Kettering Foundation that explored public opinion about scientifically complex issues that had a significant area of expert uncertainty involving a threat to public health. Moderators gave students a handout that briefly compared the four choices for approaching this problem: source reduction; recycling; incineration; and landfills.

8. As the Kettering Foundation has found, one of the six "stages" in community politics is "naming and framing a problem for public deliberation." When a problem is named in public terms – described in the same terms people use to talk about what they care about and why they care about it – they are able to grasp its day-to-day impact on their lives, and they are more likely to get involved. When a problem is named publicly, it is clear that the traditional polarized debates cannot get at the problem. A range of choices of public action must be identified that reflect all the different concerns, and must include the tensions between and among the different areas people hold valuable. For more information on the stages of community politics, see *The Basics of Community Politics* (Dayton, OH: The Kettering Foundation Press, 1998).

9. Thomas Jefferson, *Letter to William Charles Jarvis*, (September 28, 1820).

10. The issue of solid waste disposal was originally framed in a 1990 Public Agenda study for the Kettering Foundation. The goal was to explore whether the general public could engage with scientifically complex issues, even when there were significant areas of expert uncertainty, such as the actual risk to public health, or the safety of solid waste-to-energy incinerators. The students in this Doble study were told that most scientists believe well-run incinerators are safe, a minority thinks they are not, and a fair number are simply not sure.

11. The author would like to thank Dr. John Dedrick, program officer at the Kettering Foundation, for his invaluable comments and suggestions on earlier versions of this essay.

## References

Boyte, Harry C., and Nancy Kari. 1996. *The Democracy of Public Work*. Philadelphia: Temple University Press.

Cruset, Kristin. 1998. *Deliberation in the Classroom*. Dayton, OH: A Report to the Kettering Foundation.

Doble Research Associates. 1999. *The Enduring Effects of National Issues Forums on High School Students*. Dayton, OH: A Report to the Kettering Foundation.

Ford, Paul L., ed. 1903. *The Works of Thomas Jefferson*. New York: Knickerbocker Press.

Mansbridge, Jane. 1995. *Does Participation Make Better Citizens?* Paper presented at the PEGS Conference, February 11-12.

Mathews, David. 1996. "Reviewing and Previewing Civics." In *Educating the Democratic Mind*, Walter C. Parker, ed. New York: State University of New York Press.

Mathews, David, and Noelle McAfee. (1999). *Making Choices Together: The Power of Public Deliberation*. Dayton, OH: The Kettering Foundation Press.

Patrick, John J. 1999. "Concepts at the Core of Education for Democratic Citizenship." In *Principles and Practices of Education for Democratic Citizenship*, Charles F. Bahmueller and John J. Patrick, eds. Bloomington, IN: ERIC Clearinghouse for Social Studies/Social Science Education.

Perry, Michael. 1998. *Teachers' Project: Observations from Interviews in a Focus Group*. Bethesda, MD: The Harwood Group.

# 7

## Education for Citizenship: Promising Effects of the *Kids Voting USA* Curriculum

### *Steven Chaffee*

The 1990s saw a number of innovative programs aimed at reengagement of the electorate. One of the most promising is *Kids Voting USA*, a volunteer organization headquartered in Tempe, Arizona. The mission of *Kids Voting* is to help schools educate students for future citizenship roles through an innovative curriculum, mock ballots at polling places, and community events. As of this writing, *Kids Voting* is reportedly being used in all schools and polling places in the state of Arizona, and in many other local communities around the nation. This report is based primarily on evaluations conducted at the time of the 1994 and 1998 California elections in the large (but largely suburban) city of San Jose. During that period, San Jose was the only California community with a *Kids Voting* organization.

When I first discussed the evaluation with the founding leaders of *Kids Voting* in the summer of 1994, I painted a fairly pessimistic picture so that they would not hold their hopes too high. A review of the literature had confirmed my impression – dating from the 1960s when political socialization was a hot research topic – that schools could accomplish relatively little to foster citizen behaviors. My own research had instead dealt with such alternative agents as parents and the news media, and I resolved to build these factors into my evaluation. *Kids Voting* would be accomplishing something, I reasoned, if it stimulated students to follow news of the election campaign and to discuss it with their parents. I also expected some didactic knowledge would be acquired, as is true of any education program, but I did not expect to find much in the way of strengthened party identification, motivation toward voting, or age-appropriate forms of political participation such as expressing opinions on current issues or attempting to bring others around to one's own view on an issue or candidate.

The *Kids Voting* curriculum includes many exercises to engage a student in making informed choices on the political issues in a current election campaign. Early on, a class might be assigned to interview their parents about the first time they had voted, or to study a candidate or an issue on the ballot. They might be taught about the history of the vote, such as women's suffrage, laws on voting (for example, felons cannot vote, but in California the homeless can), and why people form political parties. Special projects sometimes included class discussions of a proposition, debates between or speeches by adherents of different candidates, and analysis of television commercials for candidates or ballot propositions. In San Jose a citywide "Kidsvention" was modeled on party conventions, and drew more than 1,000 student delegates. Finally, on Election Day students were urged to accompany their parents to the polls, where a special *Kids Voting* ballot box was staffed by volunteers at every polling place in the city. All these activities were thoroughly covered in local news media, including San Jose's major daily newspaper, the *Mercury News*, and the local news on its one television network affiliate.

The California election campaign in 1994 was a lively one. Not only were there closely contested races for both governor and United States senator, there were a number of divisive initiative propositions on the ballot. The one that particularly aroused students that fall was Proposition 187, which proposed several anti-immigrant policies that hit home for San Jose's many Hispanic (mostly Mexican) and Asian (mostly Vietnamese) families. Our pre-tests showed that students were talking with one another about Proposition 187 more than they were the races for either governor or senator. So we decided to feature interpersonal discussion as well as mass media attention among the indicators of political socialization in our evaluation of *Kids Voting San Jose*.

To avoid being seen as instruments of either *Kids Voting* or the schools (our study was in fact funded by the Policy Study Center of the Annenberg School for Communication at the University of Pennsylvania), we decided to interview students by phone at home. Parental permission to interview children is required by university human subjects committees, so we also decided to ask the parents the same questions (or as nearly so as possible) that we asked the students. We envisioned this parallel data as a set of "control" measures, assuming that parents who were themselves highly knowledgeable and active politically would have a powerful "intergenerational transmission" effect on their children that we would need to separate from the anticipated puny effect of the *Kids Voting* curriculum at school.

Results in 1994 were far from puny, however. My research assistants and I were nothing short of astounded at the size of the correlation coefficients that showed up on the computer screen as we examined one political socialization indicator after another. Our independent variable was the student's self-report of having been taught *Kids Voting* lessons of various sorts that fall, although only the final item in the interview mentioned the program by name. Some 40 percent of the students in our sample of families said they had been taught *Kids Voting* lessons, and another 20 percent reported school experiences very similar to those in the *Kids Voting* curriculum. A summed nine-item index representing exposure to the curriculum was uncorrelated with background factors such as the student's grade, gender, ethnicity, or school grades, and it was also uncorrelated with the parent's education, occupational level, and political affiliation or involvement. So we considered that any outcomes predicted by this exposure represented a *de facto* field experiment, as if the teachers of San Jose had inadvertently assigned students in our sample randomly to various levels of the independent variable we were studying.

These outcomes were impressive both in variety of content and strength of effect. We found significant effects on information that had been taught about voting, and somewhat stronger effects on knowledge about the candidates and issues in the California campaign. We found only slight effects on normative values related to the importance of voting, apparently due to a ceiling effect. But these were very strong effects on the strength of party identification, and on the extent to which students gave opinions when we asked them about current issues. The strength of these effects was little disturbed when we controlled for the parent's level of the same measures; intergenerational transmission correlations were in the range of $r = .10$ while effects of *Kids Voting* lessons were in the $.20 < r < .70$ range. We also discovered very strong effects on several indices of communication, including attention to the news media, and discussion of politics by students with both their friends and their families.

This last finding was validated when we checked the parents' answers to parallel questions. We discovered that not only had the curriculum stimulated students to go home and talk with their parents, but this activity had a measurable impact on the parents too. Indeed, *Kids Voting* had statistically significant effects on almost every parental indicator of political socialization we measured. For example, the more voting-related lessons a student reported at school, the more likely the parent was to identify with a political party, to express opinions on current issues, to pay attention to public affairs news in the media, and to report discussing the election with others – including neighbors and co-workers. In short, there was a statistically significant "trickle-up" effect of *Kids Voting* on parents. Later studies confirmed that the mediating activity in this process was conversations about politics that were initiated at home by the students, rather than by the parents. Thus the parent interviews provided much more than control variables and validation of the students' self-reports; we uncovered a secondary process of political socialization that had scarcely been hinted at in prior research. This was manifested in significant increases in newspaper reading, attention to news on television, expressing opinions, and party identification, in parents as well as in their children.

While exposure of students to *Kids Voting* at school was essentially randomized throughout the social structure, the effects of the program were not. They were much stronger on working class families than on the middle class. *Kids Voting* helped to close the gap between social strata, by bringing working class kids up to levels of political competence and activity commensurate with those of middle class students. It raised working class parents, who had missed out on significant political socialization opportunities when they dropped out of school short of college themselves, in the same way (if not to the same extent) – a sort of "second chance" at the political socialization they had missed the first time around.

Mock voting at the ballot box was particularly effective in stimulating student-parent interactions and consequent "trickle-up" socialization. Probably because the trip to the polling place was an occasion for talking over their voting intentions, students who carried out this added component of the curriculum were particularly likely to report parent-student discussion of politics, as were their parents. These discussions probably occurred both earlier and later than election day in some families. It should be noted that mock voting, unlike exposure to the curriculum at school, was not randomly distributed across social strata; it was more typical in middle-class families. Still, it is a feature of this curriculum that affected both students and parents in substantial ways.

Follow-up interviews of the students six months later indicated that the initial impact of *Kids Voting* had persisted well beyond the election period. For most dependent variables, effects were not as strong as they had been immediately after the program ended, but most of them remained significant and were on average about half the strength of the initial findings. *Kids Voting* students did well, for example, on a current news quiz about plans of the Republican majority that took over the Congress in 1995. (These items would not have been taught in *Kids Voting* classes the previous fall, when there was scant mention in San Jose of Newt Gingrich, the Republican leader who became Speaker of the House of Representatives following the 1994 elections.) Pro-voting norms in May were more strongly associated with the *Kids Voting* lessons than they had been the previous November, perhaps because these statements became truisms during the election, and created a temporary ceiling effect.

If the 1994-95 study provided good news on the prospects for political socialization via the *Kids Voting* curriculum, a replication in 1998-99 brought some bad news. The basic problem in 1998 was a lack of volunteers to staff the program in San Jose. As of that summer only a lone secondary school teacher staffed the office of a program whose scope had been expanded from the city of San Jose to the entire county, in effect doubling the target population in the largest city and county in northern California. Few teachers heard about the curriculum from a staff member until after it was too late to work it into the fall semester teaching plan. When we sampled families on the east side of the city – the working class area targeted for concentrated *Kids Voting* efforts based on our 1994 findings – we found that only about 8 percent of the students were exposed to the curriculum in 1998.

Nevertheless, the general pattern of effects on students in 1998 was the same as in 1994, for those who received the lessons. That is, the beta weights (see Table 7.1) were approximately the same for the major dependent variables such as attention to the campaign, party identification, political knowledge, opinion holding, news media use, and interpersonal discussion. But the serendipitous results of 1994, including both the trickle-up effect on parents and the closing of gaps in political behavior between working class and middle class families did not recur. The effects on students again persisted in our delayed evaluation six months after the election and the end of the curriculum, again in lesser degree. So at least the promise of this rich curriculum was documented a second time.

But in general the 1998-99 results were disappointing, and it was not hard to find why. An effective curriculum is only one component of a volunteer organization. People must present themselves to staff it, and that did not happen to nearly as great an extent in 1998 as it had in 1994. The Knight Foundation, which funded the 1998-99 replication, has acted on our most urgent recommendation by making an infrastructure grant to *Kids Voting San Jose*, and to a number of other local *Kids Voting* organizations around the country for the 2000 election year.

The larger lesson of these studies is that school interventions aimed at political socialization can work. Young people can be engaged with active citizenship through the excitement of an election campaign, and through the controversies aroused by ballot propositions as well as by party politics. But this takes work, both by classroom teachers and by quasi-professional staffs of organizations that design and disseminate educational modules.

*Kids Voting* is a success story, and a model for kindred agencies to emulate. It creates not just voters, but knowledgeable and enthusiastic citizens. It can engage whole families in the political process, bringing parents who might not have fully developed as citizens when they were in school themselves into the fold too. But this does not happen as a matter of course. The effort must be renewed each election year.

### Table 7.1

### Effects of 1994 and 1998 *Kids Voting* Interventions in San Jose (increments to variance explained by curriculum)

| Criterion | 1994-1995 | | 1998-1999 | |
|---|---|---|---|---|
| | Immediate | Delayed | Immediate | Delayed |
| Party identification | .03*** | .01* | .05*** | .03** |
| Political knowledge | .05*** | .00 | .06*** | .04*** |
| Attention to news | .15*** | .04*** | .09*** | .07*** |
| Opinionation | .14*** | .05*** | .05*** | .00 |
| News media use | .06*** | .02** | .07*** | .03** |
| Peer/family discussion | .09*** | .03** | .07*** | .04*** |
| (N) | (441) | (312) | (374) | (299) |

*p < .05, **p < .01, ***p < .001
Note: Cell entries are increments to variance in each criterion measure, from a hierarchical regression equation that includes controls for the interviewed parent's education, income, ethnicity, and level of the criterion variable; and the student's gender, age, and year in school.

## References

McDevitt, Michael, and Steven Chaffee. 1998. "Second Chance Political Socialization: Trickle-up effects of Children on Parents." In *Engaging the Public: How Government and the Media Can Reinvigorate American Democracy*, Thomas J. Johnson, Carol E. Hays and Scott P. Hays, eds. Lanham, MD: Rowman & Littlefield.

McDevitt, Michael, and Steven Chaffee. 2000. "Closing Gaps in Political Knowledge: Effects of a School Intervention via Communication in the Home." *Communication Research* 27 (June): 259-292.

# 8

# We the People . . . Project Citizen

## Herbert M. Atherton

*For the things we have to learn before we can do them, we learn by doing them.*
*– Aristotle*

The Center for Civic Education's *We the People . . . Project Citizen* is a case-based, problem-solving curriculum, involving an entire class, through which students learn how to monitor and influence public policy. It is one of several curricular initiatives in civic education that responded to renewed attention in the late 1980s and early 1990s to the educational needs and opportunities of middle-school students. Such blue-ribbon studies as the Carnegie Council Task Force on Education of Young Adolescents (Carnegie 1989) and the National Council for the Social Studies Task Force on the Social Studies in the Middle School (NCSS 1991) called for a reinvigorated and restructured curriculum for the middle grades, one whose teaching strategies and content themes would address the developmental needs of young adolescence, a key formative period for the student's self-identify, values, and relationship with peers, community, and the broader world.

To address these developmental realities through the social studies curriculum, the NCSS report recommended a variety of instructional practices, including experiential, interdisciplinary, and cooperative learning, the opportunity to engage controversial issues, and authentic, performance-based assessment. It emphasized the value of curricula that included concrete and familiar case-based problem-solving and group deliberation, integrated personal experience with academic knowledge, and expanded the classroom into the community through research activities and community service. "Through community service," the NCSS task force report noted, "students can contribute to their society while developing an appreciation for human dignity and diversity, a respect for rights and responsibilities, and a sense of fellowship and social justice" (NCSS 1991, 291).

*Project Citizen* takes its cue in large part from such directives. It also signals the transformation that has been taking place in civic education over
the last several decades. The didactic, "pressure-cooker" civics, born a
century ago to meet the assimilationist demands of the "new immigration" and sustained by the spirit of solidarity of two world wars and the
onset of the Cold War, was based on a view of the "good citizen" as essentially passive and spectatorial, with little emphasis on empowerment. It
gave civic education a somewhat off-putting prescriptive and didactive
quality, the vestiges of which remain to this day.

What has emerged in recent decades is a more proactive concept of
citizenship. The transformation began in the late 1960s and 1970s and
was the result of a convergence of different trends. Those years
witnessed a resurgence of volunteerism and community service seeking to address various manifestations of malaise in the nation's *civitas*,
from political alienation, disengagement, and cynicism to materialist self-
preoccupation. Concurrently, progressive education came once again into
fashion, prompted by influential work in developmental psychology. The
convergence of the new social consciousness and renewed interest in
experiential education fed the transformation of civic education.

The roots of the new civics, however, are to be found much earlier, in
the beginnings of modern civic education a century ago. First father to the
basic concept underlying programs like *Project Citizen* was Arthur Dunn,
who, in *The Community and the Citizen* (1907) and other writings, argued
the educational value of integrating the social studies curriculum with
community service. Dunn proposed a community-based civics program
for middle school. Perhaps the most influential voice in more recent times
for a proactive view of citizenship and appreciation of the central role of
civic education in overall development of the student has been Fred
Newmann (although focused on senior high school rather than the middle grades). In Newmann, developmental psychology and social consciousness converged to produce a theory of civic education as empowerment. Newmann indicted traditional civic education for neglecting "the
most crucial component in democratic theory: the right of each citizen to
*exert influence*" (Newmann 1995, 4). For Newmann, as for Aristotle, the
development of the civic self is central to the development of the whole
person.

More recently, civic educators such as Harry Boyte and James Farr
(1997) have distinguished their vision of the empowered "good citizen"
from the traditional "liberal" view of the citizen as a rights-bearing individual of a political system and from the communitarian view of the citizen as the caring member of a moral community with shared values.
Invoking traditions of American pragmatism, the authors suggest another

*ideal-type* of citizenship defined as "public work" – the citizen as a practical agent in a civic world who works together with other citizens on the tasks and problems they collectively face. If citizenship is thus defined as public work, as practical problem-solving, then civic education's primary task is to provide younger citizens with the tools of the trade. The young should "be thought of as citizens-in-the making who have serious work to do" (Boyte & Farr 1997, 43).

*Project Citizen* is very much in keeping with this model of citizenship. Its goal is to "develop students' commitment to active citizenship and governance" by "providing students with the knowledge and skills needed to participate effectively in society and the practical experience designed to foster a sense of competence and efficacy" (Tolo 1998, 107). The program is designed for use with middle- and upper-elementary school students in grades 6 to 9. The program has also been used in senior high school government courses and in classes with special needs. Funded by the U.S. Department of Education, it is now completing its fifth year as a national program. It derives from a California pilot program, the *American Youth Citizenship Project*, funded by the Walt Disney Corporation in 1991-92. During its five years as a national program (through February 2000), *Project Citizen* has reached over 3,000 teachers and almost 200,000 students. The program is administered by the Center for Civic Education (CCE) through a national network of state coordinators. With a long-standing commitment to improving education about state and local government, the National Conference of State Legislatures co-sponsors the program. NCSL has also been instrumental in securing supplemental state funding in several states.

The heart of *Project Citizen* is its problem-solving methodology. It mirrors in large measure the methodologies of other issues-centered curricula in the social studies, which are derived from the work of John Dewey. (See Dewey, *How We Think*, 1910.) It includes six sequential steps: (1) identifying appropriate public policy problems in the community through class discussion, research, interviews, media scanning, and other survey techniques; (2) selecting a particular problem among several alternatives presented in class discussion and deliberation; (3) gathering information on the selected problem through library, archival, and Internet research, interviews of government officials and civic leaders, and other research activity as suggested by the nature of the problem and community resources available; (4) developing a class portfolio and research binder to document the results of the project; (5) presenting and defending those results in a simulated public hearing; (6) reflecting on what has been learned as a result of the experience. The student text provides worksheets and checklists to assist students in completing the several stages of their project.

Teamwork becomes especially important in the fourth stage of the curriculum: developing a class portfolio. To complete this part of the project, the class divides up into four groups, each charged with a specific task. Group 1 develops an explanation of the problem. Group 2 evaluates alternative policy solutions. Group 3 develops a proposed policy, one that is favored among the various alternatives. Group 4 develops an action or implementation plan for that policy. The results of each of these group efforts are represented on one panel of the four-panel portfolio, in an array of selected text, illustration, and other appropriate documentation.

In the simulated public hearing (stage 5), the class members have an opportunity to explain and defend the results of their project before a panel of judges. This culminating assessment exercise may be informal in nature, or it may take place in a formal competition whereby *Project Citizen* classes compete at the local and state levels, usually before public officials and civic leaders in their communities who take the role of judges. The portfolios of the winning classes at the state level are then evaluated in a national competition, coincidental with the annual convention of the NCSL.

Several qualities of the *Project Citizen* curriculum stand out. The curriculum is student-driven. In order for the program to achieve its desired effects, student ownership of the project must be genuine, from the selection of the public policy issue to the preparation and defense of the project portfolio. Teachers and adult volunteers play important supportive and facilitating roles, but the work must be largely the students' own. *Project Citizen* appeals to "outgoing, flexible, innovative teachers" who "trust their kids" (Tolo 1998, 43). Teachers must show both initiative and restraint. The program also requires a measure of trust on the part of principals, superintendents, and school boards. They must allow young students to address potentially controversial issues. It perhaps says much for the integrity of the program and the enthusiasm of its participants that school administrators generally have been trusting and supportive.

Given the latitude accorded students, it is not surprising that possible topics for *Project Citizen* have ranged far and wide. Some classes decide to focus on issues within their own school community. Such projects will likely address one of a variety of educational reform issues such as student rights, dress codes, safety, overcrowded classes, or sex education and AIDS awareness. Other *Project Citizen* classes select an issue in the wider community of their town, county, or state. Such issues have ranged over several topic areas, from the environment (illegal dumping, graffiti, beautification projects) to health (substance abuse, teen pregnancy) to social pathologies (street gangs, domestic violence, homelessness) to infrastructure problems (traffic congestion, fire-fighting services).

Whatever the project issue, its focus must be sufficiently local and familiar so that students can address it effectively within the time span allowed. Students should be expected to address issues that they can investigate realistically. Their project problem may have broader, systemic dimensions, but the focus must be real and immediate. For example, if students express interest in the problems of world hunger, their teacher might encourage them to examine a manifestation of that global problem closer to home, in what their community is doing to feed the homeless or the homebound.

Because *Project Citizen* involves an entire class, and because it is student-driven, cooperative learning figures prominently in its methodology. Students work primarily in groups, for some parts of the project in plenary session as an entire class, in other parts as specialized teams, who shadow each other's work. The methodology also lends itself to cross-disciplinary opportunities. The social studies might seem the obvious and preferred context for launching a *Project Citizen* project, but the curriculum has found a home in the language arts and other subjects as well. The range of projects can take students into a variety of subject areas and can call upon the exercise of a variety of different skills. Environmental or health-related issues open up the natural sciences. Research and analysis may require mathematical and computer skills.

*Project Citizen* is grounded in the methodology of public policy analysis. As public policy analysis has evolved beyond the arcane world of academic think-tanks into a discrete sub-discipline of political science, educators have come to realize the potential of this methodology in civic education, integrating theory and practice, civic knowledge with civic skills, in a problem-solving, real-life context. Parker and Zumeta (1999), for example, have suggested that the essential elements of public policy deliberation (PPD) provide an appropriate methodology for teaching of proactive, democratic citizenship at the high school level. Albeit in simplified form, the various steps of *Project Citizen* mirror these same analytical fundamentals: the toolbox, as it were, for young citizens engaged in pragmatics of public and community service.

Young though it still is, the domestic impact of *Project Citizen* has been evaluated in two national studies. A year-long study by the Lyndon B. Johnson School of Public Affairs at the University of Texas (Tolo 1998) examined all aspects of the program, from administration to classroom impact. Measuring the outcomes of *Project Citizen* by means of teachers and student surveys as well as other evaluation instruments, the study made several key findings, all suggesting that the program achieves what it is intended to achieve. Teachers surveyed noted the simplicity and logic of the curriculum, its inclusiveness, integration of various disciplines and skills, and concrete results. The study documented the benefits of the program in several areas, including increased knowledge of public policy, government, and community service, as well as the fostering of research, communication, and teamwork skills. But perhaps most compelling was evidence that *Project Citizen* was an engaging educational activity that empowered young citizens and gave them a sense of that empowerment. Students, the LBJ study found, not only believe they can make a difference as citizens in their communities – they frequently *do* make a difference. The investigation of low-voter turnout by a California *Project Citizen* class led to changes in voter registration procedures in their county and state. The Michigan students whose action plan articulated a policy to deal with sexual harassment in their school saw that plan's adoption by the local school district. "I learned," said one *Project Citizen* alum, "that no matter how old you are, you can make a difference just by taking action" (Tolo 1998, 108). "I have had students," one *Project Citizen* teacher observed, "come back and tell me how it changed their lives" (Tolo 1998, 111).

In 1999 the National Staff Development Council endorsed *Project Citizen* as one of three social studies programs that effectively boosted student learning in the middle grades (Killion 1999). The NSDC review committee looked for programs that "promote challenging and thought-provoking experiences for students through strategies such as research, small group work, problem-solving, and simulations to construct an in-depth understanding of issues and processes that are directly related to the world beyond the classroom" (Killian 1999, 137). The NSDC endorsement singled out *Project Citizen* for its high level of student participation, cultivation of higher order thinking skills, and portfolio-based assessment strategies. It also recognized *Project Citizen's* value to the professional development of teachers in promoting their understanding of public policy and government and enhancing their repertoire of content-specific instructional strategies.

Though some anecdotal and tell-tale evidence suggests that students who participate in community-outreach programs like *Project Citizen* are more likely to vote and become involved in community service in later years, longitudinal studies will be necessary to measure the lasting effect in terms of civic engagement (Niemi 1999). An assessment of the *Project Citizen* curriculum is now part of a School Violence Prevention Demonstration Project, implemented by the Center for Civic Education with Department of Education funding, to test the effectiveness of CCE programs in dealing with some of the early warning signs of troubled youth. The program's effectiveness will be measured by attitudinal surveys in selected school districts across the country.

Given *Project Citizen's* emphasis on the generics of public policy and civic engagement, it is not surprising that the program has traveled well overseas. Indeed, it has proved to be one of American civic education's leading exports to the countries of eastern and central Europe, where fledgling democracy has brought with it a rejection of authoritarian pedagogies and a keen interest in models for teaching proactive citizenship.

In the last few years pilot programs have been launched in several republics of the former Soviet Union (including the Russian Federation) and in most of the countries of the former Soviet bloc, from the Baltic Sea to the Balkan Peninsula, where the curriculum has been adapted to local needs and translated into local languages. *Project Citizen* has realized some of its most dramatic success in the strife-torn countries of the Balkans. A pilot program in Bosnia/Herzegovina using *Project Citizen* (and CCE's *Foundations of Democracy* curriculum) has involved over 134,000 students and 4,400 teachers in the first four years since its implementation. An evaluation of the instructional impact on students of the pilot program is nearing completion.

During this last academic year (1999-2000), a *Project Citizen* program was initiated in Ireland, as part of a major educational effort to strengthen ties between Northern Ireland and the Republic of Ireland in the wake of the 1998 Good Friday Agreement. Sponsored by an NGO, Co-operation Ireland, as its *Civic-Link* program, *Project Citizen* is bringing classes of students from north and south together, working in tandem on a common project through collaborative research and residential visits.

*Project Citizen* has also established a foothold in Latin America, including Brazil and Mexico. Seven Mexican states participated in the 1999-2000 year program. Initiatives are underway in the Middle East and in the Far East as well. Despite obvious cultural differences with schools and communities in the United States, the issues selected in these international programs have been remarkably similar, suggesting perhaps a universality of interests and a range of common public policy issues everywhere. Many of the *Project Citizen* issues on which foreign students have focused invoke the same social, economic and cultural themes, from environmental pollution to traffic congestion to drug abuse, that have drawn the interest of their American counterparts, which suggests a perennity and even a universality of interests about local public issues (Hepburn 1997).

The flexibility of the *Project Citizen* curriculum has allowed it to travel generationally as well as geographically. It has provided a basis for recent initiatives of the Center for Civic Education in higher education. During the current academic year (1999-2000), CCE launched pilot tests of a *Project Citizen Mentor Program*. The program will be expanded in academic year 2000-2001 as part of a grant from the Corporation for National Service to the American Association of Community Colleges. Analogous in some respects to the University of Colorado's Presidential Leadership Program and to initiatives of the Public Achievement Program at the University of Minnesota, this new venture links undergraduates to *Project Citizen* classes as mentors. In general, mentors act as facilitators to the younger students through the various stages of the project, and, in many instances (depending on academic interests and specialization), they also serve as expert resources for background information related to the project. Mentoring provides a service-learning opportunity for courses in political science, sociology, teacher education, and other subjects. CCE is also developing a more sophisticated version of the *Project Citizen* methodology as a supplemental text for other service-learning opportunities in undergraduate education.

The realization of *Project Citizen's* potential, in fact, may depend in part on its convergence with service learning, which has established itself in recent years as an attractive refinement of experiential education and has been gaining moment at both the collegiate and pre-collegiate levels of American education. As with community service and experiential education generally, the rationale of service learning is closely associated with ideas of "civic responsibility" and "civic engagement." More often than not, however, the precise educational goals embodied in such rhetorical phrases have gone undefined, and without reference to the particulars of a meaningful and effective civic education curriculum. Soup kitchens are not civics – not in the absence of strategies for developing the knowledge, skills, and dispositions of citizenship. Westheimer and Kahne (2000), for example, have documented the uneven academic quality of service learning programs.

Is *Project Citizen* a service-learning program? It depends on how narrowly or broadly service learning is defined, on what are considered realistic service-learning opportunities for middle schools, and on the specifics of a given *Project Citizen* project. The curriculum does not fit the classic definition of service learning with its emphasis on experiential learning in the context of community service (i.e., working with as well as for the beneficiaries of a particular service in the community). *Project Citizen* is essentially a classroom/community outreach activity, emphasizing public policy analysis and civic participation.

Nonetheless, the curriculum embodies many of the same instructional strategies and objectives that have come to be associated with service learning. Like all service-learning pedagogies, *Project Citizen* emphasizes the interplay of reflection and experience. In addition to a concluding reflective exercise, the curriculum throughout encourages students to test their preconceptions with experience and to revise the former in the light of the latter. A critical step in the policy analysis of *Project Citizen*, for example, requires students to articulate and evaluate alternative solutions to the project problem. This step encourages analysis, judgment, and deliberation, and it engages students with normative as well as empirical issues, allowing them to examine not only their own values, interests, and preconceptions, but those of others as well.

Like service learning, *Project Citizen* places great value on collaborative endeavor and the sharing of ideas. Like service learning, it emphasizes the importance of the authenticity of the learning experience: the projects are ones the students in large measure choose themselves. Finally, *Project Citizen* embodies a key element of the ethos of service learning: democratizing the school environment. *Project Citizen* is an inclusive, collaborative learning experience that endorses democratic values in the learning process and encourages students to confront issues of concern to their school as well as to the larger community. It signals that even younger students have something to say and deserve to be heard in matters concerning their education. Like service learning, the program is as much a mindset as it is a pedagogy, a mindset that "helps democratize our schools and communities by giving voice and influence to young people who are often the recipients of service, but are rarely asked to be 'of service'" (McPherson & Kinsley 1995, 115).

Whether or not the program meets all of the particulars of a service learning litmus test, *Project Citizen* affords students experiential learning in the public policy process by "doing" the process themselves and by bringing them into contact with officials and institutions involved with public policy and government. Depending on the nature of and time allotted for the class project, the program brings students into contact with a variety of other community resources as well. Because the community outreach opportunities of *Project Citizen* has proved to be so attractive to students (Tolo 1998, 110), evidence thus far suggests that many students follow through afterwards with volunteer service in the community.

At the very least, then, *Project Citizen* provides an ideal springboard to community service and service-learning opportunities, by establishing community partnerships and by equipping students with the prerequisites for effective service. And it provides one model of how such learning opportunities, if well grounded in the appropriate frames of reference and equipped with the appropriate learning tools, can prepare younger students for democratic citizenship.

## References

Boyte, Harry C., and James Farr. 1997. "The Work of Citizenship and the Problem of Service Learning." In *Experiencing Citizenship: Concepts and Models for Service Learning in Political Science*, Richard M. Battistoni and William E. Hudson, eds. Washington, DC: American Association for Higher Education, 35-48.

Carnegie Council on Adolescent Development. 1989. *Turning Points: Preparing American Youth for the 21st Century: The Report of the Task Force on Education of Young Adolescents*. Washington, DC: Carnegie Council on Adolescent Development.

Dewey, John. 1910. *How We Think*. Boston: D.C. Heath.

Dunn, Arthur William. 1907. *The Community and the Citizen*. Boston: D.C. Heath.

Hepburn, Mary A. 1997. "Service Learning in Civic Education: A Concept with Long, Sturdy Roots," *Theory into Practice* 36 (Summer): 136-142.

Killion, Joellen, Mary McFarland et al. 1999. *What Works in the Middle: Results-Based Staff Development*. Washington, DC: National Staff Development Council.

McPherson, Kate, and Carol W. Kinsley. 1995. "Conclusion: Challenges for the Future." In *Enriching the Curriculum through Service Learning*, Carol W. Kinsley and Kate McPherson, eds. Alexandria, VA: Association for Supervision and Curriculum Development, 115-116.

National Council for the Social Studies. 1991. "Social Studies in the Middle School: A Report of the Task Force on Social Studies in the Middle School." *Social Education* 55 (September): 287-293.

Newmann, Fred M. 1975. *Education for Citizenship Action: Challenge for Secondary Curriculum*. Berkeley CA: McCutchan Publishing Corporation.

Niemi, Richard G. et al. 1999. "Community Service by High School Students: A Cure for Civic Ills?" A paper prepared for presentation at the annual meeting of the American Political Science Association, September 1-5.

Parker, Walter C., and William Zumeta. 1999. "Toward an Aristocracy of Everyone: Policy Study in the High School Curriculum." *Theory and Research in Social Education* 27 (Winter): 9-44.

Tolo, K.W., ed. 1998. *An Assessment of We the People . . . Project Citizen: Promoting Citizenship in Classrooms and Communities*. Austin, TX: Lyndon B. Johnson School of Public Affairs at the University of Texas.

Westheimer, Joel, and Joseph Kahne. 2000. "Service Learning Required: But What Exactly Do Students Learn?" *Education Week:* 19, 20, 52 and 32.

# 9

# Working to Improve Civic Education: The Dirksen Congressional Center

*Frank H. Mackaman and Andrea Schade*

*Our challenge and responsibility are clear. If we would desire good citizenship, love of country, respect for heritage among our young, then we must teach them. And we must do so actively, consistently, and most of all early. It is essential that we provide children with an environment conducive to the learning about, practicing of, and valuing of good citizenship and responsible involvement in national life.*
*— Everett McKinley Dirksen, 1967*

Part of the answer to getting students involved in their communities is to first get them involved in their classrooms. The social studies classroom, whether it be history, government, or civics, is the perfect platform for teaching students the importance of becoming active in the world around them. When it is boiled down, those subjects teach about people taking action. Educators have a natural opportunity to teach students ideas and information and how to make use of them for the public good. Social studies also emphasizes the importance of public opinion, but unfortunately students are too often asked merely to sit and listen.

Just as active participation and public opinion are important aspects of well-managed classrooms, they have become a key to the success of The Dirksen Congressional Center's educational programs. The Center, chartered in 1963 but opened for business in 1975, is a nonprofit, nonpartisan educational and research organization devoted to the study of Congress — its leaders and members, its structure and processes, and the public policies it produces. Named for the Senate Minority Leader in the 1960s, Republican Everett McKinley Dirksen, the Center is located in his home town of Pekin, Illinois.

## CongressLink

CongressLink <www.congresslink.org> is The Dirksen Center's largest investment in educational programming. Work on CongressLink began in 1996 with a survey of teachers, assessing their needs for Internet-based lessons in the classroom. We determined that teachers were eager to investigate the educational possibilities of the Internet but were somewhat intimidated by the vastness of the World Wide Web. Travel ahead four years to 2000, and CongressLink has evolved into an internationally recognized web site which serves teachers and students of government, civics, and history. The site employs technology-based approaches to instruction and cutting-edge services that enhance civic education. It also offers information, lesson plans, primary source documents, and communication tools to help users gain a deeper understanding of the legislative branch. The overarching purpose behind CongressLink is to improve the woeful lack of understanding of our government so convincingly documented by recent National Assessment of Educational Progress test scores among American students. See the NAEP data on Civics and U.S. History by visiting this World Wide Web site: <http://nces.ed.gov/nations report-card>. The categories of information in CongressLink are illustrated in Figure 9.1 at the end of this chapter.

CongressLink's features can be divided into three categories: information, lesson plans and resources, and communication tools. The concentration of general information is located in the "Know Your Congress" section. Here users will find a roster of the current congressional leadership, information about congressional procedures, and historical facts and figures. Direct e-mail and web page links for Congress members are available, as are committee lists and congressional pay rates. Students can also find the name and contact information for their Representative and Senators. Especially popular during the Clinton impeachment proceedings was information on past Senate cases of censure and condemnation.

The bulk of CongressLink materials consists of lesson plans and related resources. CongressLink has a growing library of lesson plans, the majority of which were written by teachers. Lesson topics include Congressional Workload, Congressional Powers, the Veto Process, Teaching the Amendments, the Compromise of 1850, and the Job of a Congressman. All lesson plans use CongressLink and are based upon the structure of Bloom's Taxonomy, which defines learning objectives in several categories. Applicable national civics standards are also listed with each plan. The template for CongressLink lesson plans is available online, and The Dirksen Center encourages teachers to submit original lessons.

Associated with the CongressLink lesson plans are resource documents such as the U.S. Constitution, Washington's first State of the Union Address, and congressional leadership statements. CongressLink's version of the Constitution is unique in that it is hyper-linked to the Con-gressLink glossary and historical notes. If students are confused by con-stitutional terms, such as "enumeration" or "advice and consent," explanations are just a mouse click away. CongressLink also features a selection of civil rights documents from Everett Dirksen's archival collec-tion. Letters, press releases, newspaper clippings, and speeches relating to the Civil Rights Act of 1964 help students understand the history behind the legislation and give meaning to the law-making process.

CongressLink's communication tools are the least used sections of the site but perhaps hold the most potential. The CongressLink message board allows teachers and students to post ideas, questions, and lesson plans to share with colleagues and peers. The message board can expand a teacher's world and knock down the four classroom walls that often hinder communication and creativity. One of the goals for CongressLink is that eventually teachers will post lessons to the message board and other educators will add their own suggestions for the plans. The Dirksen Center then would combine the ideas and post a final version to the les-son plan section of CongressLink.

Teachers also use the message board to confer with one of Con-gressLink's Experts Online. An Expert Online is a subject matter specialist who has agreed to communicate with classes and answer questions from them. Teachers have the opportunity to contact a congressional staff member, a journalist, or a number of scholars who can give students first-hand knowledge about the subjects they are studying. For example, seventh-grade students at an American school in Saudi Arabia posted questions about congressional-presidential relations on the message board. The Dirksen Center arranged for political scientist Charles O. Jones to respond to the questions, and the answers were posted for the students to read. What a beneficial experience for students in the Middle East to be able to correspond with a leading political scientist in the Midwest!

An often-used feature of CongressLink that does not fit easily into any of the above-mentioned categories is Related Web Sites. Since Con-gressLink does not and cannot contain every bit of information about Congress, the site provides links to over seventy-five other government, political, and civic education web sites. Each listing is annotated to help users save time when searching for information.

CongressLink is becoming increasingly recognized among teachers and other educational web sites. This was not always the case, however. The site suffered a slow start, so The Dirksen Center turned to educators to ask how CongressLink could be improved. A number of teachers deserve credit for helping give CongressLink a new look, making the fea-tures easier to navigate, contributing practical classroom content, and training colleagues to use the site. What The Dirksen Center has learned is that it needs teachers to make CongressLink a success. Not just teachers as users but teachers as contributors. Who knows better what is needed in the classroom than teachers?

The continuing collaboration with teachers has made CongressLink a successful and worthwhile classroom tool. Since we began counting users in August 1998, over 1.5 million hits have been recorded. The site is free, easy to access, and rich in practical materials. Teachers can obtain traditional classroom resources – lesson plans and primary source documents – and at the same time incorporate new technology such as web links and message boards. Indeed, the National Center for Educational Statistics has identified use of the Internet as a factor leading to higher civic literacy test scores. Best of all, CongressLink is driven by the needs of teachers and students, and we hope that one day users will be able to customize the site to best fit their needs. CongressLink provides materials that teach about our government and also gives users a tool to voice their opinions, ask questions, and contact their political leaders. This is teaching democracy, not just teaching about it.

## Congress in the Classroom®

"This program has no fluff. It's all core-based, substantive information that will truly help me in my teaching career. I'm in awe as I look over these past three days and realize what I've been exposed to." A Congress in the Classroom® participant in 1997 offered this typical testimony about the worth of Dirksen Congressional Center programs.

The Dirksen Center's longest running program for educators, Congress in the Classroom®, is a free summer workshop for secondary teachers and junior and community college instructors of history, government, civics, and political science. Congress in the Classroom® encourages the exchange of ideas on Congress by bringing together educators and experts for a three-day conference. During the program, teachers hear from presenters on a range of historical and current topics. Past speakers have included scholars, journalists, members of Congress, archivists, and teachers.

As education has evolved over the years, so has Congress in the Classroom®. The topics of discussion change to keep up with timely issues, and the methods of presenting information to the participants change as well. Traditional lecture sessions by the experts are typical, but in the past three years we have also incorporated some interactive, technology-related sessions involving CongressLink and "Congressional Insight," a computer simulation of the job of a Congress member. These activities help create a participatory environment for the teachers.

This environment is enhanced by the interaction among those who attend Congress in the Classroom®. The small number of participants allows for sharing of lesson ideas and teaching techniques with colleagues from across the country. And beyond the classroom sessions, participants often are able to converse with the speakers during breaks and meals. Discussions with experts in the lecture hall and at the dinner table have a lasting effect on the participants and on what they share with their students. Teachers hear about how Congress works from those who work with Congress, and they leave with a greater appreciation for the difficult and complex job facing legislators.

## Robert H. Michel Civic Education Grants

In too many cases social studies is the last area of curriculum to receive attention and funding. The Dirksen Center addresses this problem by sponsoring the Robert H. Michel Civic Education Grants.

An annual total of $45,000 is available to teachers and developers of history, government, social studies, and political science curricula. The grants encourage individuals to create lessons and projects that incorporate web sites, historical materials, or simulation exercises that teach about our federal government and the importance of civic responsibility. Other eligible proposals include projects that identify innovative teaching resources, reform efforts designed to bring instruction in line with civic education standards, and university-level methods curricula for preparing educators to teach about government.

The Michel Grants have helped to fund a national American government web design contest, an Internet course which teaches about the relationship between legislatures and interest groups, and the purchase of multi-media editing software used to conduct a student-led voter participation program. This is not a complete list of projects funded by the Michel Grants, but this sampling shows how the program has helped to rejuvenate civics-related curriculum and make it more relevant and interesting to students. These are activities that minimize passive note-taking in class and maximize participation in learning.

In the future The Dirksen Center would like to incorporate many of the grant products into our other programs. William Ball of the College of New Jersey used a Michel Grant to create a web site which contains a catalogue of 500 images associated with American political history. All of the photographs are uncopyrighted and available for classroom use. Teachers could integrate the images into CongressLink lesson plans, using The Center's investment in one program to strengthen another.

## Collaborative Projects

Increasingly The Dirksen Center collaborates with other entities to offer programs or products. Two examples are "Congressional Insight" and *Congress and the Decline of Public Trust.*

"Congressional Insight," a product of the National Association of Manufacturers, is a computer simulation that puts participants in the place of first-term members of Congress. Players are faced with realistic day-to-day decisions. Whom should they hire for staff? Which candidate should they back for party caucus chair? Should they spend time fund raising, intervening on a constituent matter, or going to a committee meeting? Participants receive feedback on their choices, and if they handle the various demands and please enough of the right people, they are re-elected.

Not only does "Congressional Insight" give participants a greater appreciation for the job of a Congress member, the simulation also helps groups develop a better understanding of the political process, build decision-making skills, and improve teamwork. The Dirksen Center has experienced success in presenting the program to a variety of audiences including students, teachers, and political action committees.

The Dirksen Center has sponsored several publications relating to Congress, the most recent being *Congress and the Decline of Public Trust* (Boulder, CO: Westview Press, 1999). This collection of nine essays analyzes the current state of distrust in our government and suggests reasons for it. Authors comment on how the media, the education system, members of Congress, and Congress as a whole can be part of both the problem and the solution. The book contains one essay of special interest to teachers, "Congress, Public Trust, and Education."

Success in The Center's educational programming depends on involving our audiences. Whether it be asking for help in improving CongressLink, giving teachers the opportunity to interact with experts during Congress in the Classroom®, or providing assistance for developing innovative curricula with the Michel Grants, The Center's programs engage those whom they serve. Perhaps implementing the same practice in the classroom would result in informed and active students who want to make a difference in their communities. The Center's web site <http://www.pekin.net/dirksen>contains up-to-date information about its programs and services.

## Figure 9.1

## CONGRESSLINK

### Table of Contents

*CongressLink provides new ways to learn about Congress, how it works, its leaders and members, and the public policies it produces. Select* <u>About This Site</u> *for more about CongressLink's purpose.*

| | |
|---|---|
| Know Your Congress | Basic information about Congress and how to contact your representative and senators |
| Resources for Teachers | Tips for using the site, templates for lesson plans and assessments, suggestions for what students should know about Congress |
| Resources for Lesson Plans | U.S. Constitution (with hyperlinks to definitions and historical terms), historical documents, primary sources, and narratives to serve as resources for creating lesson plans |
| Lesson Plans and Student Activities | Developed by teachers using CongressLink on topics such as how a bill becomes law, congressional leadership, checks and balances, civil rights, communicating with Congress members, and constitutional amendments |
| Experts Online | Scholars, teachers, journalists, and Congress people who have agreed to consult with you about Congress and teaching |
| Related Web Sites | Annotated list and links to more than 75 Web sites about Congress and civics |
| Communications | Online conferences (i.e., bulletin boards and chat rooms) about CongressLink and how teachers use it |
| About This Site | Site philosophy, developers, National Lead Teachers |
| Register | Stay in touch with CongressLink developments by registering |
| Search This Site | Search CongressLink using key words |

# 10

# The Public Service Academy

## John G. Stone III

A public service academy is a school-within-a-school, having a public service career theme (government and non-profit sectors). The school-within-a-school setting usually requires a cohort of teachers and students to teach and learn together over the three or four years of high school. The academy setting includes establishing high academic expectations for students, course work related to the public service theme, out-visits to partners' work places and colleges, and student involvement in work-based job shadowing and internships.

### What Are the Basic Elements of the Academy?

The basic elements of the program combine both student and teacher motivation, college preparatory studies, experiential learning, and expanded resources:

1. Teachers choose to be in the academy, and are willing to participate in extensive staff development and team planning and teaching.
2. Students choose to be in the academy, through a recruiting process involving entrance requirements – a combination of grades, behavior, and interest. Frequently a written contract is signed by the parents as well as the student, which sets forth expectations and commitments.
3. Students and teachers develop a secure learning community, where each knows the others personally, where the values are traditional and positive, and where there is mutual support.
4. Non-school partners from the public service community provide support and contributions to the students and teachers, such as:
   - Expert help with the career curriculum, loaned public executives for academy managers, volunteers for various projects (such as debate, speech and essay contests) and as mentors and tutors, help in meeting individual student non-academic needs, reaching

out to the wider community, program evaluation, and members of the steering and working committees.

- Financial support: fund raising, donations, organizational sponsorship, and scholarships.
- In-kind donations: organizing and paying for events like a graduation ceremony and field trips, awards, busses, computers and software, training and internships for teachers and students, college visits, SAT preparation courses, printing, supplies, and a tax exempt bank account for receiving non-school funds.
- The presence of the larger community in the lives of the students, and specific evidence of their worth to society.
- Support and encouragement for teachers and administrators;
- Connection to the government and the public service community in their city, county, state and nation.
- Public recognition of the academy and the school.
- Advice to administrators and teachers on management and related matters.

5. Teachers and partners plan together and deliver a curriculum that combines college preparatory education and employability training. The goal is to give every student the option upon graduation of going to work or entering college.

6. Teachers are encouraged to teach in teams, using an integrated approach to delivering the curriculum across traditional lines. Students learn to work in teams in a project-based curriculum, in the manner of the working world.

7. Out-of-school instructional activities relating to their classroom work give students direct personal experience of work places and college campuses.

8. Students are exposed to college students and older adults who care about them and support their development. The adults provide role models, help students become comfortable in the world outside the neighborhood, and often serve as mentors and personal guides beyond high school.

9. Students are encouraged to be school leaders, engage in sports and other extra-curricular activities, provide for self-government, and participate in the development of the program, often through representation on the steering committee.

## What Are the Objectives and Outcomes of the Academy?

Often the objectives of the program are set forth in the memorandum of understanding, signed by representatives of the school district, school partners, and non-school partners. The memorandum of understanding for the Public Service Academy at Anacostia High School in Washington, D.C., for example, sets forth the following objectives:

- To stimulate students to stay in school and graduate.
- To inculcate the values of good citizenship, constructive employment, and public service.
- To prepare students for higher education and jobs in government and other public service organizations, and increase the rate of graduates who go on to college.
- To expose students to many places where higher education and public service work are done.
- To provide a center for expanding public service education at the junior high and elementary school levels, and a School of Distinction to attract students from throughout the District of Columbia.

The learning outcomes defined by the teaching team at Anacostia High School address skills (reading, writing, speaking, mathematics, research, problem solving, decision making, technology, employability, and working cooperatively in groups) and exercising the rights and responsibilities of good citizens in a democratic society.

### Why Is the Out-of-School Program So Important?

At many academies the work based component and the college visits have proven to be a primary reason for student success. They are attractive ways to learn, and they provide students a laboratory for applying and expanding their learning. More importantly, they give students the personal experience of work places and college campuses.

Job shadowing and internships during the summer and school year give students an opportunity to work closely with supportive adults who are committed to public service, and to develop the role model and mentoring relationships that can be helpful later. They provide a transition to the world after high school and a first-hand experience of government.

Associating with college students and instructors, and visiting campuses, provide information about college entrance and financial aid, demystify the world of higher education, and give academy students an opportunity to see their own potential for being there. Internships for teachers are common. They facilitate aligning classroom instruction with industry practices and culture.

### How to Get This All Into a School Day?

Integrating the in-school and out-of-school elements of the program can expand significantly the students' learning opportunities, without adding much to the course schedule. With school systems increasingly setting higher academic standards and requirements for graduation, and adding community service requirements, there is little time in the school day to add many subjects or courses.

Some relief can be obtained by accelerating completion of required subjects in grades 10 and 11 to provide time for internships in grade 12. Also helpful are getting accreditation as electives for some of the non-traditional activities of the academy, and team teaching that covers more subject matter in a scheduled period. But integrating the in-school and out-of-school elements of the program is the only way to expand substantially the student learning opportunities.

Such integration occurs (a) when academic subjects are enhanced by such out-of-school experiences as requiring written and oral reports on internships or designing field trips to include scientific or mathematical learning, and (b) when employability and civic values are taught as part of the classroom instruction, such as using business grade software in computer classes and laboratories, and requiring library research before an out-of-school activity. Not only is student learning expanded by such integration, but it also stimulates more active student participation in the instructional program, and brings the community into the school.

**What Are the Results?**

The purpose of the academy is to improve student performance, and increase the graduation and college attendance rates. With their combined academic and employability training and their interaction with adults, academy students graduate with the capacity to succeed in work and post-secondary education. Career academies have spread across the United States largely as a grass-roots movement, and every community has anecdotal and statistical evidence of their academy's success in meeting these goals.

Formal evaluation studies have followed. The Manpower Development Corporation published in February 2000 the results of the first phase of a major longitudinal evaluation of ten career academies across the nation, including the Public Service Academy at Anacostia High School in Washington, D.C. Among the findings were that career academies (1) substantially increased the level of interpersonal support for students; (2) reduced dropout rates by nearly 50% among students at high risk of school failure, and improved their attendance, credits toward graduation, and preparation for both college and work; (3) produced a 75% positive impact on students of medium and high risk; but (4) did not produce any change in standardized math and reading achievement test scores, and actually hindered low risk students from completing steps necessary to apply for and be accepted by colleges.

A recent study by the RAND Corporation points to academy students out-pacing their non-academy counterparts in more credits earned toward graduation, higher grade point averages, and an average school attendance of 20 days more per year.

## Needs and Pitfalls

The foregoing describes an ideal academy, and even the most effective of the academies does not meet every criterion fully – or sustain its capability to do so over its entire life. These programs are demanding of students, teachers, school administrators, and partners. As the academy program matures in a school, ups and downs are inevitable. Maintaining high standards, continuity of program activities, and high levels of support and commitment is a constant challenge, and sometimes a constant struggle.

Turnover in school district superintendents and administrators, in principals and teachers, and even in partner representatives is inevitable, and can be devastating. School staff not on the academy faculty can be envious and antagonistic. Enrollment pressures can lead to (1) eliminating the self-selective assignment of students and teachers, and a critical mass of people who do not want to be there, which can undermine the program, (2) assigning too many students to an academy, which prevents development of the learning community, (3) depriving the teachers of needed time to plan and coordinate the program, and (4) assigning new teachers who do not understand the academy approach

The lack of adequate support to the teaching team (the absence of a director, a manager, and clerical support) can overburden and burn out the teachers. The lack of enough cash for out-of-pocket expenses can prevent the out-of-school program from functioning. Failure to establish the necessary relationship with outside partners can reduce their participation, which not only reduces resources, but eliminates one of the most attractive features for students. The temptation to return to school as usual is constant. Successful academies find ways to meet these challenges, usually by concentrating on the basics: the interest of the students, their need for a learning community, and the importance of their exposure to the world they will enter after high school.

## How Can I Learn and Do More?

The public service academy model offers an excellent opportunity for

non-school partners to contribute to improvement of America's secondary school education, to help motivate high school students and teachers,
and to prepare young people for careers in public service. It also offers a
stimulant to the partners' organizational development and employee participation in a valuable community service.

Several efforts are underway in various parts of the country to expand
further the career academy movement. The American Society For Public
Administration (ASPA), with 120 chapters covering every state, has
joined with the National Career Academy Coalition (NCAC) in a partnership to advocate public service academies and form PSANET, a national
network of public service academies, of which two dozen have been identified. The NCAC is a grass-roots, non-profit group dedicated to assisting
existing and emerging academies with a variety of career themes. A particular initiative of NCAC is public service academies.

For further information about public service academies, and how individuals or groups can participate, contact the ASPA web page at
<www.aspa2aspanet.org> or e-mail NCAC PSANET Coordinator Tom
Schaffer at <tom@ncacinc.org>.

# 11

# Why Should the Young Desire a Career in Government or Consider Running for Office?

*Susan A. MacManus*

*Too many times, our education systems have stressed the importance of increasing scores in more measurable subjects such as math, science, and reading, all at the expense of civics. In doing so, we fail to honor this nation's original public education intentions – creating responsible citizens within a democracy.*
> – Brent McGoldrick
> Project Director
> Neglection 2000[1]

*Sad to say, when young Americans are asked to picture themselves in government careers . . . they envision dead-end jobs where seniority, not performance, rules.*
> – Paul Light
> The Brookings Institution[2]

*If you say you're going into public service, people will say: "Great!" If you say you're going into politics, they say "Why?"*
> – Collin O'Mara, College student[3]

*Note to civic engagement types: If you want to involve the younger generation in politics, don't treat it as an interest group to be soothed and stroked, but as a community of serious citizens prepared to respond to a challenge.*
> – E. J. Dionne Jr., Columnist, The Washington Post[4]

Polls, studies, focus group data, and editorials abound delineating the potential threat to democracy if today's youngest generation remains as disinterested in working in government or someday running for public office as it appears to be. Who is to blame? A study sponsored by the National Association of Secretaries of State (1999) puts the largest portion of the blame on "adult leaders in our major institutions."[5] But *all* those mentioned share some responsibility for the younger cohorts' "distrust, disinterest, and ignorance" of government.

Who is to blame is a less interesting question than *"Who can do the most to reverse this trend and how can it be done?"* In this article, I argue that the most effective intervention often comes from teachers and public officials once they are made aware of the deficiencies of high school and college civics/government courses. Two of the most blatant deficiencies are (1) the failure to inform students about the wide range of exciting jobs available in government and (2) the absence of political figures in classrooms and on campuses.[6] Ours is the first survey to document the extent to which these activities are missing from most government classes, particularly at the secondary school level.

Asking students to critique both the substance and delivery of materials covered in their government class is a vital first step in seeking answers to the crucial questions posed in this article. We asked 191 college students right out of high school to identify "the good, the bad, and the ugly" aspects of their civics class instruction.[7] We also reviewed a number of other surveys of young adults to gain a more in-depth understanding of their perspectives and to put our own findings in a larger national context (National Association of Secretaries of State 1999). The general consensus is that most high school government classes overemphasize "book-learning," are "boring" to students, and are "largely disconnected from current events" (NASS 1999, 44-45). Specifically, they focus too much on national-level politics, how a bill becomes a law, and the three branches of government, often using a purely historical approach (MacManus 1999; NASS 1999).

## Student Assessments of Civics/Government Classes

Large numbers of college students report learning very little about the "how tos" of voting in high school. As shown in Table 11.1, they say they had little interaction with elected officials, candidates for office, or professionals discussing government as a career option. They also learned little about how to get involved at the grassroots (local) level and readily admit that they were taught *next-to-nothing* about neighborhood associations, cities, counties, and school boards. Ironically, there are more jobs and more political office options at the state and local levels than at the federal level. These governments closer to home also handle public policies and services that most heavily impact the younger generation. The bottom line is that most leave high school never having been exposed to the exciting possibility of a career in the public sector or thinking about serving their community via elective office someday.

## Table 11.1

## Frequency of Topics Covered in High School Government Classes

(Responses are listed in descending order
based on the "never" response.)

| Topic | Never % | Some % | Fairly Often % |
|---|---|---|---|
| How to change voter registration | 68 | 24 | 4 |
| How to volunteer in a political campaign | 63 | 25 | 8 |
| The role of neighborhood associations | 60 | 28 | 7 |
| How to vote absentee | 60 | 28 | 7 |
| How to complain to government officials about local problems | 52 | 34 | 9 |
| How to join a political party | 52 | 35 | 9 |
| What school boards do | 48 | 36 | 11 |
| What counties do | 47 | 39 | 9 |
| What cities do | 44 | 42 | 10 |
| **How to run for office** | **44** | **40** | **12** |
| **What types of careers are in government** | **42** | **39** | **13** |
| How to sign a petition | 42 | 43 | 10 |
| How to register to vote | 37 | 45 | 14 |
| The role of lobbying in politics | 35 | 42 | 18 |
| Why people don't vote | 33 | 41 | 21 |
| The role of media in politics | 30 | 43 | 23 |
| Voting as a civic duty and citizen's responsibility | 24 | 49 | 23 |
| Political ideologies – what's liberal or conservative | 20 | 51 | 25 |
| Study of taxes | 18 | 54 | 23 |
| Difference between general election and primary election | 18 | 56 | 21 |
| How government and economy are related | 16 | 49 | 32 |
| Difference between Republicans and Democrats | 10 | 52 | 32 |
| Study of political history | 10 | 41 | 46 |
| Study of Court system | 9 | 39 | 46 |
| Study of Congress | 5 | 41 | 49 |
| Study of Presidency | 5 | 37 | 54 |

Note: The row totals may not add to 100% due to rounding or the exclusion of missing data.

Source: Survey of students enrolled in introductory political science courses at the University of South Florida, Tampa; conducted by the author, Fall, 1998.

## Government as a Career Option

Today, the private sector is more of a magnet to the young than the public sector. For many, working for government is simply not as "cool" or alluring as the possibility of making millions like mega-entrepreneurs Bill Gates or Steven Jobs. Even among young people who are more committed to making social improvements than money, nonprofit agencies offer more hope for effecting change than a government job (Dionne 2000).

Paul Light (Brookings 1999) takes governments at all levels to task for having neglected career development. He argues that government hiring, firing, and promotion processes are slow, antiquated, and out-of-touch with today's young work force. If changes are not made "to build a civil service relevant to a new generation of talent, [governments] will take a flying leap into an empty talent pool, sending public confidence in government even lower," says Light (2000a, 23).

Schools can play an important role in sparking student interest in a public sector career. But waiting until they are in college is not advisable since many young people do not continue their education after leaving high school. All too often, career-oriented activities at both the high school and college levels do not include any discussion of public sector employment opportunities. Consider the following two scenarios:

Scenario 1
It's the annual Great American Teach-In at a local high school. Those appearing in the classroom include a newscaster, stockbroker, several small business owners, college professors, a lady wrestler and a race car driver (no kidding!), lawyers, a grocery chain manager, and several emergency room nurses, and doctors to name a few. Glaringly absent is anyone from government – line employee, manager, or elected official.

Scenario 2
At a college across town, it is Career Day featuring exhibits, videos, and real live persons ready to "sell" their profession and/or corporation to future graduates. The same pattern is evident here – no one is present promoting careers in the public sector.

This is not uncommon. Our survey showed that over 40% of young college students say no one ever came to talk to them about government career options when they were in high school. Would that have interested them? *Yes.* Twelve percent said such information would be a meaningful addition to high school government or civics classes.[8] In fact, as shown in Table 11.2, it was among the eight most common recommendations offered by the students via an open-ended question format.

## Table 11.2

## Student Recommendations on How to Redesign
## High School Government Class

| Ways to Redesign High School Government Class | | Column % |
|---|---|---|
| | More student-teacher interaction | 38 |
| | **Bring in elected official or political candidate as guest speaker** | **25** |
| | Discuss the importance of voting | 21 |
| | Require course during senior, not freshman, year | 21 |
| | More focus on state & local governments | 20 |
| | Make it more fun to learn about/look at current events | 17 |
| | Less bias/more objectivity from teacher/let student make up own mind | 18 |
| | **More information on types of careers in government** | **12** |
| | More discussion of political parties & ideologies | 12 |
| | More discussion of voting processes (the how tos) | 11 |
| | More class/group projects | 11 |
| | More class discussions and debates on issues | 11 |
| | Choose teachers who are enthusiastic about politics | 11 |
| | Hold mock elections, straw polls, mock trials, mock constitutional conventions | 10 |
| | Make class two semesters, not one | 10 |
| | Select more interesting text books | 8 |
| | Arrange for more opportunities to volunteer | 6 |
| | More discussion on presidency | 6 |
| | Teach where to find information about candidates | 5 |
| | Require students to summarize newspapers | 5 |
| | Smaller classes | 5 |
| | Do not combine class with other subjects, especially history | 3 |
| | Learn more about Dept. of Defense or Chiefs of Staffs | 2 |

Source: Survey of 191 students enrolled in introductory political science courses at the University of South Florida, Tampa; conducted Fall 1998 by the author. These are responses to an open-ended question. The column percentages add to greater than 100% due to the multiple response question format.

## Selling Government Careers: New Forms of Media Must Be Used

Groups like the National Association of Schools of Public Affairs and Administration (NASPAA) have joined hands with others to try and reverse this alarming trend – the shrinking government talent pool. With funding from the Pew Charitable Trust, the "Calling Students" campaign features advertisements, print materials, and a web site. The somewhat slap-stickish "Look Ma! I'm a Bureaucrat" production focuses on true stories of nine *young* public service professionals ranging from age 24 to 36. They are shown performing jobs that seem to be anything but "bureaucratic" in nature (Director of NASA's Computer Crime Division, Lead Public Affairs Officer for the Federal Emergency Management Agency, Global Climate Change Advisor to the U.S. Department of Energy, to name a few of those featured).[9]

"Letting the young talk to the young" is an effective strategy. It is more convincing for someone from their own cohort to promote the notion that choosing to work in the public rather than the private or nonprofit sectors does pay off.

Using media that is "with it" makes good sense as well. Studies have clearly shown that politically oriented messages and advertisements are far too infrequently tailored to the young.[10]

Increasingly, government officials are turning to the young to help them develop more media-savvy informational campaigns aimed at younger constituents – via the Internet as well as "in-person." An excellent example is the "Get Out The Vote" team created by the Supervisor of Elections in Pinellas County (St. Petersburg), Florida. The "Gen X" team goes into all county high schools to register seniors, conduct mock elections, and answer questions about the mechanics and importance of voting. The team is composed of three college students who are members of Pi Sigma Alpha, the National Political Science Honor Society, at the University of South Florida. The students planned the outreach program. An attention-grabbing poster featuring caricatures of the three students was designed and drawn by a young county employee and placed in all the high schools announcing the team's arrival. It has been a highly successful venture, according to all involved.

## The Excitement of an Elected Official in the Classroom or on Campus

Getting young elected officials into the classroom is an equally effective way to spark interest in voting and in running for office. The declining candidacy rate of young people, particularly at the local level, has already been documented.

One of the oldest adages in politics is: "If you meet a candidate in person, the chance that you will vote increases considerably; the odds you will vote for that candidate also goes up markedly." Unfortunately, this wise old saying appears to have been forgotten by far too many educators – administrators and teachers – and elected officials. A scant 9% of the students surveyed reported that their high school government teacher ever invited an elected official into their classroom. Just 7% said their teacher ever brought in a political candidate and had them talk about what it is like to run for office.

Some school districts and principals actually ban candidates from visiting schools. Such "no politics on campus" policies and other attempts to cleanse campuses from politics (often for partisan or ideological reasons) are neither healthy for democracy nor fair to students. A more desirable approach is the one articulated in the midst of the Election 2000 campaign cycle: "There is a point when you have to put your partisanship aside in order to get our children to understand what our political process is. And I would think that most parents are thrilled – Democrat or Republican – that their children can experience [a presidential candidate coming to their high school]" (Scripps Howard News Service 2000).

The sad thing is that few young people ever have the chance to meet *any* elected officials in person, let along a presidential contender. As the costs of campaigning escalate and the number of senior-age voters increases, candidates target the elderly more than younger voters. (See Figure 11.1 at the end of the chapter.) Critics of this approach argue that "Candidates tend to go where the money is rather than to where the future is" – the future being younger generations (Scott 2000).

Relatively small percentages of high school and college students have had an opportunity to meet an elected official or hear candidates in person. It is easy to understand why presidential contenders cannot make it to many schools. It is less comprehensible why many local officials rarely visit the schools in their own backyards anymore.

Left to rely on media-molded images of elected officials, young people today subscribe to the notions that all politicians are corrupt; it takes a pot-load of money to win office; media scrutiny is too intrusive; and one cannot make a difference even if elected. Gen-Xers assume anyone who wants to run for public office is crazy. But of course they have little knowledge of why people run for office and whether it is a manageable exercise. When given the opportunity, the young are anxious to find out: how old the candidate was when she/he first ran; who prompted them to run; what personal satisfaction they got out of it; how much it costs; how much time it takes; and what the position pays.

## Finding Out That Elected Officials Are Real People, Too!

The Hillsborough County, Florida Supervisor of Elections was invited to speak to an Introduction to State and Local Politics class at the University of South Florida. I asked her to make a brief statement about her entry into elective office. She proceeded to tell the class how she decided to run for county commission at the urging of her father and a few friends. Without much money, but with lots of volunteers and a campaign headquarters in her kitchen, she proceeded to win at 26 years of age – becoming the youngest county commissioner ever elected to public office in the Tampa area. After being term-limited, she decided to run for Supervisor of Elections and won that, too.

In their written analyses of the Supervisor's presentation, nearly every student in the class mentioned two factors: her age when she first got elected and the fact that she won with hard work, not just tons of money.

Students who have been fortunate enough to have interacted with elected officials and candidates in their classrooms are almost twice as likely to hold open the possibility of running for office someday. (See Table 11.3.) Bringing dynamic young local elected officials into classrooms, particularly those who ran strong grassroots campaigns, helps eliminate stereotypes about running for office that are generally formed from watching media coverage of national-level campaigns (Rosenthal et al. 1999).[11]

### Table 11.3

### Meeting an Elected Official Increases Chances of Running For Office

% within Elected official to class

|  | | Would you want to run for office someday? | | | Total |
|  | | Yes | Maybe | No | |
|---|---|---|---|---|---|
| Elected official | Yes | 16.7% | 50.0% | 33.3% | 100.0% |
| to class | No | 13.6% | 27.2% | 59.3% | 100.0% |
| Total | | 13.9% | 29.4% | 56.7% | 100.0% |

Source: Survey of students enrolled in introductory political science courses at the University of South Florida, Tampa; conducted in Fall 1998 by the author.

## Young See Same Problems/Issues as Old But Have Different Perspectives and Priorities on How to Resolve Them

Several things politicians do are particularly offensive to young people:

talking down to them, treating them as if they have no in-depth knowledge of or opinions about issues, and/or assuming they are only interested in education.

It is a well-established fact that younger cohorts focus more on a candidate's issue stances than on his/her character, the reverse of older age groups.[12] To the young, it appears that all the media care about are candidate backgrounds and the horse-race dimension of a campaign. One high school senior from Virginia Beach has some sage advice for journalists: "We need to somehow get the media to move away from their delight in argumentative, polarized politics and substanceless scorekeeping" and get them to cover the issues in more depth (Waller 2000).

There is a tendency to assume that the *only* issue of major concern to younger voters is education. However, surveys asking Americans to identify the most pressing problems confronting the nation or their community reveal a fairly high level of agreement among the young and the old. They tend to identify the same problems as being the most serious. Where the generations differ is in their views on what are the causes of the problem, how to remedy them, and the order in which they should be tackled. (See Figure 11.2 at the end of the chapter.) These differences are largely a product of where they are in the life cycle. If elected officials, political candidates, and government civil servants do not interact with young constituents – either in the classroom, in the community, or at the workplace – they will continue to hold "conventional wisdom" that ultimately is neither conventional nor wise.

### Recommendations

I have shown the importance and urgency of recruiting more young people to jobs in government and enticing more of them to run for public office. I have also shown that public officials and educators can play a huge role in making sure these things begin to happen. I offer these suggestions to educators:

What should educators – administrators and teachers do?

- Eliminate policies that prohibit candidates from coming to schools.
- Invite more public sector professionals, elected officials, and political candidates into your classroom, especially younger ones; try your best to bring in representatives of the various political parties.
- Make sure Career Days include young professionals from government.
- Hold mock elections and straw polls; invite election personnel to conduct these elections using standard equipment and ballot formats.

- Engage students in more issue-related debates and group formats.
- Have students design public opinion surveys and political ads that would appeal to younger voters; share them with local officials and media.
- Make better use of the Internet to study how campaigns are conducted and how candidates present themselves; have students rate the effectiveness of web-sites – style, substance, links, etc.
- Avoid an exclusive focus on national-level elections and issues.

What should teachers ask of public officials who visit the classroom/campus?
- Share the details of why you got into politics, and what you find most challenging and rewarding about it.
- Give students some insights into your campaigns – your age when you first ran, how much it cost, who helped you, etc.
- Discuss your use of the Internet as a means to communicate with your constituents (web sites; links; chat rooms).
- Talk about exciting, rewarding careers in government: examples, pay, educational requirements, how to apply, etc.
- Make yourself available for interviews with campus newspaper/TV reporters.
- Invite a student(s) to "shadow" you for a day.
- Invite our students to participate in the "fun" parts of politics (barbecues, debates, rallies, fund-raisers, party conventions) as volunteers and/or participants.
- Attend more student-sponsored candidate forums and mock elections.
- Promote Student Citizen and Government Days (for example, mock city and county commission meetings; school board meetings; mock United Nations sessions; mock court activities).

This is not an exhaustive list, by any means, but it is a start. The challenge is to "cultivate reasoned, active, and informed citizens." "Without such a citizenry, our democracy is at risk," says the executive director of the Florida Law Related Education Association.[13] We cannot create such a citizenry if we continue to exclude public sector officials and politicians from our classrooms and campuses.[14]

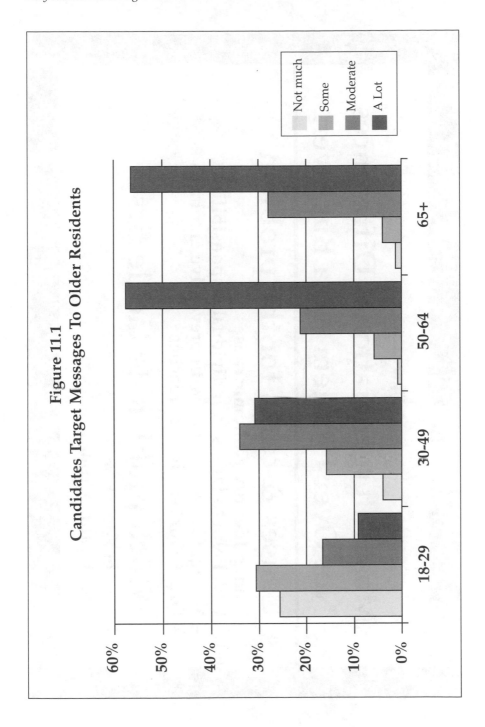

Figure 11.1
Candidates Target Messages To Older Residents

Figure 11.2

# Most Intergenerational Differences Not Over Problem Area But Over:

## • Causes & cures for the problem

- – Young: Identify economic causes
- – Old: Point to lapses in individual responsibility
- – Young: Favor solutions with preventive emphasis
- – Old: Favor reactive approaches

## • Which problem to tackle first

- – Young: Education
- – Old: Health, Crime

## Notes

1. Neglection 2000 is designed "to bring attention to the cycle of mutual neglect that, we hypothesize, exists between presidential campaigns and young adults (age 18-24)." Using surveys, focus groups, and political advertising analyses (message; placement), the project will monitor the outreach efforts of presidential candidates. The author sits on the advisory board for this project.

2. Paul C. Light, "The Empty Government Talent Pool: The New Public Service Arrives," *The Brookings Review* 18 (Winter 2000): 20-23.

3. Quoted by E. J. Dionne, Jr., "Preferring Policies Over Politics," *Washington Post National Weekly Edition*, January 30, 2000, 22.

4. Ibid.

5. The study was based on a telephone survey of a random sample of 1,005 15-to 24-year-olds conducted in November 1998.

6. Many studies have asked students a wide range of questions about what is wrong with the content of government classes and instructional techniques. (See study by National Association of Secretaries of State, 1999). Our survey is the first to ask about the presence of government officials in the classroom.

7. The survey was administered in introductory political science classes at the University of South Florida, Tampa, the state's second largest public university, in the Fall, 1998 semester. Students (n=191) from some 32 states were included in the survey. The results closely mirror national surveys when similar questions are asked.

8. The figure would probably be considerably higher if the question had been asked in a close-ended format. It was asked in our survey via an open-ended question.

9. Michael Brintnall and Kathryn Newcomer, "Calling Students to Public Service Careers," April 1999: <www.naspaa.org/publicservicecareers/facts.htm>. The nine featured range in age from 24 to 36.

10. For an excellent discussion of this, see The Third Millennium. *Don't Ask, Don't Vote: Young Adults in the 2000 Presidential Primary Season*. New York: The Third Millennium, April, 2000.

11. This report, while focusing on interns, discusses the mistrust and misinformation that people have about state legislators.

12. See MacManus, *Young v. Old*; numerous surveys by The Pew Research Center For The People & Press; Third Millennium, *Don't Ask, Don't Vote*.

13. Annette Boyd Pitts, letter to Rosemary Dupras, dated June 1, 1999.

14. The author acknowledges the assistance of David Engelson, Graduate Assistant at the University of South Florida, in development of this chapter.

## References

Dionne, E.J., Jr. 2000. "Preferring Policies Over Politics." *Washington Post National Weekly Edition*. January 30.

Light, Paul C. 2000a. "The Empty Government Talent Pool: The New Public Service Arrives." *The Brookings Review*. 18 (Winter): 20-23.

Light, Paul C. 2000b. *The New Public Service*. Washington DC: The Brookings Institution.

MacManus, Susan A. 1998. "Seniors in City Hall." *Social Science Quarterly* 79 (September).

MacManus, Susan A. 1999. "What Florida College Students Say They Didn't Learn in Their High School Government Class." *The Journal of the James Madison Institute* (May-June): 4-10, 28.

National Association of Secretaries of State. 1999. *New Millennium Project; Part 1: American Youth Attitudes on Politics, Citizenship, Government, and Voting.* Lexington, KY: NASS.

Rosenthal, Alan, John Hibbing, Karl T. Kurtz, and Burdett Loomis. 1999. *A New Public Perspective on Representative Democracy: A Guide for Legislative Interns.* Denver, CO: National Conference of State Legislatures.

Scripps Howard News Service. 2000. "California School Turns Away Bush." *Press Journal* 4 (March 2).

Scott, James. 2000. "Barbara Bush Stumps for Son in Rock Hill." *The Herald*, February 9.

Waller, Alexis. 2000. "Reader's Forum: Politics 101: Students (and Adults) Get a Lesson in Stumping." *The Virginian-Pilot*, March 9.

# 12

## Building Trust in Representative Democracy

*Jan Goehring, Karl Kurtz, and Alan Rosenthal*

*There is but one method of rendering a republican form of government durable, and that is by disseminating the seeds of virtue and knowledge through every part of the state by means of proper places and modes of education and this can be done effectively only by the aid of the legislature.*

*— Benjamin Rush*

"State legislators can contribute to a much-needed improvement in the quality of civic education by sharing their experience and explaining America's tradition of representative democracy to the next generation of voters," says Massachusetts State Senator Richard Moore. State legislators are especially qualified to help students understand their roles and responsibilities as citizens.

That is why the National Conference of State Legislatures and lawmakers across the nation are joining together to launch a new civic education initiative: The Trust for Representative Democracy.[1] Based on the ideas and fundamental principles set forth by the framers of the Constitution, the Trust is designed to engage young people and build their understanding and support for America's democratic institutions and counter the recent heightened cynicism and distrust of the legislative process. America's Legislators Back to School Day, a program of the Trust, is designed to teach young people what it is like to be a state legislator: the processes and the debate, negotiation, and compromise that are the very fabric of representative democracy. These programs will build relationships between legislators and citizens to bring the process and the people closer together.

## Cynicism Prevails

While skepticism is a normal and healthy characteristic in a democracy, distrust and cynicism are a danger. In the quarter of a century since Watergate, distrust and cynicism have grown and become the dominant orientation that Americans have toward their political institutions, and particularly toward their legislative bodies. People no longer trust government to do the right thing; they are critical about elected public officials who are supposed to represent their interests; and they feel that the legislative system as it operates is wide open to special interests but not to the public. The political system gets low marks from most Americans.

Congress and state legislatures are not perfect. But neither are they broken, not according to the relevant research findings of congressional and state legislative scholars. They are better equipped, more open, more ethical, more engaged, and more responsive than they used to be. They are also more burdened, more pressured, more partisan, and more political. The realities are by no means completely positive, but they belie the perceptions that prevail today.

As a result of the current climate, talented and concerned people are discouraged from running for public office. While they may be willing to sacrifice income and even family life for public office, they are not willing to risk their reputations in an environment that is too accusatory.

## How Cynicism Arose

It is little wonder that the public is so negative. Given the environment since Watergate, it would be surprising if many people had positive views of the political system. All citizens see or hear is critical of the elected public officials and institutions that govern.

The media, as principal storyteller about politicians and political institutions, bear considerable responsibility. News by its traditional nature contains what is bad and wrong; not what is good and right. Since 1975, according to a study by The Center for Media and Public Affairs and commissioned by the Council for Excellence in Government, three out of every five television episodes involving the American political system have portrayed it as corrupt.

The widespread use of government as a target in political campaigns also undermines public trust. All too often, candidates – incumbents and challengers alike – run not only against one another, but against the political system and everybody in it.

Interest groups also contribute to the problem. Today's groups – whether single issue or multi issue – are insistent on achieving all, or practically all, of their agenda items. Groups are convinced of the right-eousness of their cause, so something must be wrong within the system (for example, legislature) if they do not prevail in the process or get every-thing they feel they deserve.

Add to all this the significant societal changes that have taken place and the culture wars that have broken out in America. While expectations of what government can do have risen, notions about why and how government should perform have become more heterogeneous and conflicting. Ethnicity, race, gender, sexual preference and attitudes toward the family, abortion, drugs, and immigration polarize opinions now more than in the past. Political institutions are caught in the crossfire.

In a nation with 7,424 state legislators and 535 members of Congress, thousands of issues, and hundreds of thousands of transactions, some-thing is bound to go wrong – to be illegal, unethical, unseemly. One can find rotten apples in every barrel. The rotten apples get virtually all the attention, and people generalize from the rotten apples to all the apples in the barrel. They do not generalize from their own legislator, whom they tend to like and reelect, to all legislators; rather, they generalize from the legislator who gets into trouble to all of those who do not.

No particular incident, specific charge, single newspaper story or tele-vision portrayal makes a huge difference, but years of battering have eroded support for the political system. Younger generations are more affected, in that their social trust, as well as their political trust, is dimin-ished. They express overwhelmingly cynical views, and they cite their cynicism as reason for indifference to and disengagement from politics.

## Civic Education

Civic education may be approached in various ways. One approach is to increase civic knowledge; a second approach is to promote civic engagement; and a third approach is to shape a civic orientation. Empha-sis in the United States tends to be on the first or second approach, with relatively little attention paid to the third.

**Civic Knowledge.** The 1998 Civics Report Card, based on the National Assessment of Educational Progress, found that two-thirds of the stu-dents at grades 4, 8, and 12 performed at a basic level, but that only one-quarter reached the level designated "proficient" (Lutkus et al. 1999). The civic educational objectives of the school system are designed mainly to increase civic knowledge. The question can be posed as to how successful public education has been in meeting this objective. The question can also be posed as to whether increased civic knowledge would serve to reduce public distrust and cynicism.

Much of the civic education conducted by legislatures is principally concerned with providing knowledge, the need to inform citizens about the three branches of government and how a bill becomes a law. The types of information that have been at the core of much of the legislative civic education enterprise may well come across as static, to adults and school-children alike.

**Civic Engagement.** Social studies teachers and schools are promoting participation, especially voting and advocacy. The North Carolina Civic Education Consortium[2] and *Project Citizen*[3] exemplify efforts to foster civic engagement by students in middle and high schools. The former has as its goal promoting democracy by getting students to deliberate, negotiate, organize, persuade, listen, and advocate. *Project Citizen*, among other things, teaches middle school students how to deal with public policy problems in their community and how to get elected officials, from school board members to legislators, to adopt their solutions. (See Chapter 8.)

Civic education by state legislatures is also turning to the activation of citizens. Legislatures are doing this by providing online access through web sites to information on bills and bill status. The Hawaii Legislature, for example, has set up a "public access room," with computer terminals and a staff to assist individuals on lobbying strategies. Increasingly, legislators are producing and distributing videos bearing the message that students ought to get involved. Idaho is an example. In 1997 it produced a video, which was scripted to focus on student actors lobbying a bill in the legislative process. Titled "Saved By the Bill," this video was designed to encourage young people to become involved.

If people participate, the civic engagement approach maintains, they will have a commitment to and become positive about the political system. That may or may not be the case, however. Orientations and engagement can operate independently of one another, as Figure 12.1 suggests.

## Figure 12.1

| Orientation | Engagement High | Low |
|---|---|---|
| Positive | (1) *Supportive Participants* | (2) *Accepting Citizens* |
| Negative | (3) *Dissident Activists* | (4) *Disaffected Dropouts* |

*Supportive Participants*, who are both positive and engaged, are few in number. *Disaffected Dropouts*, who are negative on both dimensions, are large in number. However, *Accepting Citizens*, those who do not engage but nonetheless have some confidence in the system, are many fewer than there used to be. Twenty-five years ago people might have been skeptical, but they still were relatively trusting. *Dissident Activists* have grown in numbers. They are highly engaged, but negative nonetheless; for example, those who zealously espouse one point of view, but who have little sympathy for the politicians or political institutions that never give them as much as they believe their cause merits.

Some evidence is already available to support the argument that engagement does not affect orientation. One study for example, shows no relationship between political involvement and approval of Congress and its members or favorable attitudes toward government.

*The Star Ledger*/Eagleton Poll[4], conducted in late September 1998, asked a series of questions about what New Jerseyans thought of politicians in the state. Most felt they went into politics for personal gain rather than public service. Two thirds of the respondents thought politicians looked out for their own interests while in office. Those surveyed said politicians paid only some or little attention to those who elected them when deciding what to do. And many felt elected officials were corrupt.

The same poll asked several questions about participation in the community. Community involvement does not seem to make a difference in what New Jerseyans believe about why people go into politics, what motivates them once they are there, and how much attention they pay to their constituents. However, people who attended a public meeting in their community were more likely than others to believe that fewer rather than more politicians were corrupt.

Civic engagement does not tend to make people more positive, but it does encourage people to express their views, advocate, lobby, and increase the demands on the legislature. These demands are legitimate, but so are competing demands – and no legislature can satisfy everyone. What if after encouragement to engage, and after working at advocacy, the legislature does not respond favorably to demands, or not favorably enough? How will people feel then – more trustful and supportive or more cynical and critical?

**Civic Orientation**. Currently the political system is loaded with demands from interest groups and interested individuals. The demand side is far more heavily weighted than the support side. What the system needs is greater balance, which means more support, not more demands. Therefore, civic orientation – how people perceive representative democracy – has to be changed. The perceptions that Americans have of legislators and legislatures do not reflect the reality of actual practice and performance. Nor do they accord with how the system ought to work. What is needed is more balanced and accurate views of politicians and political institutions.

## A New Public Perspective on Representative Democracy

NCSL and two other groups – the American Political Science Association (APSA) and the Center for Civic Education (CCE) – embarked in 1999 on a multi-year project to offer civic education on representative democracy to students and citizens of all ages.

The first task of the project was to figure out the message to be conveyed about how representative democracy ought to work and how it actually does work. This led to the development of a message that counters the prevailing cynical perceptions of today. *A New Public Perspective on Representative Democracy* (Rosenthal et al. 2000) outlines the prevailing public perceptions and offers a new perspective on each as follows:

1. *The Prevailing Public Perception*: Legislators are simply out for themselves, lack integrity, and act unethically.
   *The New Public Perspective*: Despite a few rotten apples in the legislative barrel, the overwhelming number of legislators are out to promote the public welfare, as they and their constituents see it. Moreover, they are generally ethical, although not everyone agrees on just what is and is not ethical in public life.
2. *The Prevailing Public Perception*: Legislators do not care what common people think, but are servants of interest groups and those who contribute to their campaigns.
   *The New Public Perspective*: Legislators care more about what their constituents want and need than perhaps anything else. No one is denied access or a hearing. But groups that have sizeable memberships or are major employers in their districts tend to have more influence than individuals alone.
3. *The Prevailing Public Perception*: People agree on what is right and what is necessary. Thus, they see no good reason for legislators and the legislative system not to implement such consensus.
   *The New Public Perspective*: People in our diverse and pluralistic system do not agree on issues except at a general level. It is the job of the legislature to resolve the clash of values, interests, and claims.
4. *The Prevailing Public Perception*: The values and interests of the average individual are not represented.
   *The New Public Perspective*: Americans are represented directly or indirectly by interest groups as well as by legislators. Legislators are

dependent on the groups' good will and votes. Nearly eight out of every 10 Americans are members of an organized group, and many belong to multiple groups. In politics, sheer numbers count, but those who are vocal and intense also have influence.

5. *The Prevailing Public Perception*: The legislative process is unworkable because of politics, unprincipled deal making, and needless conflict.

    *The New Public Perspective*: The process is contentious because it encompasses different and competing values, interests, and constituencies, all of which are making claims on government or one another. Some differences are fought out, but most are negotiated, compromised and settled – at least to a degree and for a while.

6. *The Prevailing Public Perception*: The political system and politicians are not accountable.

    *The New Public Perspective*: Legislators who run every two or four years, who may be subject to recall and whose every vote is on record, are as accountable as anyone could be.

The authors of the new perspective (Rosenthal et al. 2000) have drafted it into a legislative intern guide. Twelve states (California, Delaware, Georgia, Kansas, Kentucky, Maryland, Massachusetts, Minnesota, Missouri, Ohio, Utah and Washington) tested the guide through their intern programs in the 2000 legislative session. The guide has been used differently in the twelve states and evaluations and anecdotal evidence are being collected on the guide's effects. In a more formal study, the Donahue Institute at the University of Massachusetts will be doing pre- and post-tests with legislative interns who use the guide and, as a control, those who do not.

A revised version of the guide will be used in the twelve states and also distributed to the other states by the fall of this year for interns in the 2001 sessions. The legislative intern guide also has been revised for use by social studies teachers in high schools.

The "New Public Perspective" does not suggest that representative democracy in the states and nation is a perfect system. It is in need of continuing improvement. Currently our political institutions are trying to figure out how campaigns can best be financed: so that candidates have enough money to get their messages to citizens, corruption is minimized, a role continues to be played by political parties, people can know who is giving to whom, and free speech is observed. Unfair campaigning, the intrusion of campaigning into the legislative process, and extreme partisanship are also problems with which legislators have to come to grips. Achieving these objectives is no simple matter, but demonizing the political system is not a healthy approach.

**Countering Cynicism**

The best way to affect people's perceptions of legislators and the legislative process is to bring people and the process closer together. Given the negative involvement, as long as legislators and legislatures are remote and abstract, it will be easy for people to be distrustful and cynical. The operating principle here is that familiarity breeds empathy, not contempt.

The NCSL sponsored America's Legislators Back to School Day seeks to build relationships and trust between legislators and students, teachers, and parents. NCSL's partners in this project include the Center for Civic Education, the American Association of School Administrators, the National Association of Elementary School Principals, and the National Association of Secondary School Principals. Six states (Arizona, California, Iowa, Massachusetts, Ohio, Nevada) participated in the pilot project on September 17, 1999. The program was a resounding success, reaching thousands of students. The program will be rolled out to all fifty states this year and will become an annual event on the third Friday in September.

The event is designed to teach students what it is like to be a state legislator – to put kids in the shoes of a legislator. The purpose of this day is not to teach about the three branches of government or how a bill becomes a law but rather to help students understand the pressures, conflicts, and difficulties that legislators deal with in trying to solve public problems. Back to School Day will promote the "New Public Perspective on Representative Democracy" to help achieve these goals. NCSL has developed resource materials and products to aid in this effort that include:

- A generic video produced by NCSL will show how people disagree on issues and how legislatures have to work things out. Vignettes familiar to students will illustrate disagreement, deliberation, negotiation, and compromise in order to reach a settlement.
- Suggestions for simulations or games that the legislator can conduct in class will, for example, require groups of students to play the role of representatives and decide on an issue, with students assigned positions on the issue and varying distributions of constituency opinion.
- An illustrated brochure, including the principal points of the "New Public Perspective on Representative Democracy" that is aimed at teachers, administrators, students, and parents is being developed for distribution.

Building links between state legislators and the future voters and leaders of the nation will improve understanding of how representative democracy works, help to dispel cynicism, and strengthen trust in the political process.

## Notes

1. The Trust for Representative Democracy, <http://www.ncsl.org/public/trust.html>.

2. North Carolina Civic Education Consortium, <http://ncinfo.iog.unc.edu/programs/civiced/index.html>.

3. Center for Civic Education, Project Citizen, <http://www.civiced.org>.

4. *The Star-Ledger*/Eagleton Poll, Release 70-7, October 18, 1988.

## References

Center for Media and Public Affairs. 1999. *Government Goes Down the Tube: Images of Government in TV Entertainment*. Washington, DC: Center for Media and Public Affairs.

Hibbing, John R., and Elizabeth Theiss-Morse. 1995. *Congress as Public Enemy: Public Attitudes Toward American Political Institutions*. New York: Cambridge University Press.

Lutkus, Anthony et al. 1999. *The NAEP 1998 Civics Report Card for the Nation*. Washington, DC: U.S. Department of Education.

Rosenthal, Alan, John Hibbing, Karl Kurtz, and Burdett Loomis. 2000. *A New Public Perspective On Representative Democracy: A Guide for Legislative Interns*. Denver, CO: National Conference of State Legislatures.

# Appendix A

## Guide to Resources on Civic Education through Service Learning

*By Andrea Roufs, Ann Treacy, and Rob Shumer*

This annotated bibliography is intended to direct educators to resources that relate to civic participation and service learning. The resources have been separated into five sections: (1) General Discussion, (2) Research, (3) Curriculum, (4) Program Examples, and (5) Organizations. Some of the General Discussion pieces presented are instructional in nature, while others give a theoretical or historical background to the relationship between service learning and civic engagement. The brief Research section looks at literature on the effects that service learning has had on the development of social responsibility, civic identity, and moral-political awareness in students. The Curriculum section provides information about instructional materials that have been developed for elementary through high-school aged students, while the Program Examples section lists resources that discuss specific programs but do not provide curriculum materials. The last section, Organizations, lists and provides contact information for organizations that are involved in service learning, many of which have an emphasis on civic engagement.

The following bibliography includes items in the database of ERIC (Educational Resources Information System) and the database of the Learn and Serve America National Service-Learning Clearinghouse. ERIC is part of the U.S. Department of Education's National Library of Education. The ERIC system consists of sixteen clearinghouses, each of which acquires current education-related materials for the ERIC database in specific subject areas (e.g., social studies/social science education). The ERIC database contains records consisting of citations with abstracts for two types of materials: education-related journal articles and education-related documents such as policy papers, state curriculum guides, conferences presentations, research reports, teaching units, and lesson plans.

The journal articles are prefaced in the following bibliography with an EJ number. The other items have an ED number.

ERIC records may be accessed in several ways. Public Internet access to the ERIC database is available through the World Wide Web, telnet, and gopher sites. In addition, the ERIC database is available at many large public and university libraries. For more information contact ACCESS ERIC at (800) 538-3742 or visit the system-wide ERIC World Wide Web site at <http://www.accesseric.org/inex.html>.

The full text of many of the items with ED numbers in this bibliography may be purchased from the ERIC Document Reproduction Service (EDRS) at (800) 443-ERIC or <service@edrs.com> or <http://edrs.com> accessed at ERIC document microfiche collections available at many major libraries, or ordered from commercial publishers. Journal articles listed in this bibliography can be found in journal collections of major libraries, purchased from article reprint services such as CARL Uncover S.O.S. and ISI Document Solution, or obtained through Interlibrary Loan services.

The following bibliography is a small but representative sample of the great number of materials on service learning and civic education in the ERIC database and the database of **Learn and Serve America National Service-Learning Clearinghouse**, which is located at the University of Minnesota, R-460 VoTech Building, 1954 Buford Avenue, St. Paul, MN 55108-6197; Fax: (612) 625-6277; Telephone: (800) 808-7378; E-mail: <serve@tc.umn.edu> World Wide Web site: <http://umn.edu/~serve>.

*1. General Discussion*

**ERIC No:** EJ548161
**Title:** Four Perspectives on Service Learning and Citizenship Education.
**Author:** Barber, Benjamin R.; And Others
**Publication Date:** 1997
**Journal Citation:** Social Studies Review; v36 n2 p7-9 Spr-Sum 1997
**Abstract:** Presents four brief essays expressing the importance of combining service learning and citizenship education. Authors Benjamin Barber, Joan Schine, Harry C. Boyte, and James C. Kielsmeier stress the advantages of learning democratic concepts and principles, as well as understanding civic government, through student participation.

**ERIC No:** EJ554733
**Title:** Service Learning and Democratic Citizenship.
**Author:** Battistoni, Richard M.
**Publication Date:** 1997

**Journal Citation:** Theory into Practice; v36 n3 p150-56 Sum 1997

**Abstract:** The content, skills, pedagogy, and structure that should guide the design of service-learning curricula for citizenship education are examined. For service learning to teach youth about their responsibilities as citizens in a democratic society, content and strategies must model and support democratic principles.

**Title:** Citizenship Education and the Public World.
**Author:** Boyte, Harry C.
**Date Published:** 1992
**Pages:** 6
**Notes:** From a roundtable at the annual meeting of the Amer. Pol. Sci. Assoc. (Chicago, IL, Sept. 3, 1992). See also title "Going to the Community".
**Availability:** Civic Arts Review v5 n4 p4-9 Fall 1992

**Abstract:** Boyte argues that civic education should be designed so more students reflect on their lives and careers in ways that allow them to integrate their concerns with larger arenas of governance and policy, and help them to understand and develop their capacities to act effectively in such arenas as well as in their everyday environments. The concept of public is much more useful than community in accomplishing such reflection. Boyte contrasts his opinions to those of Benjamin Barber, John Dewey, and Robert Kegan.

**ERIC No:** ED408204
**Title:** Educating Tomorrow's Valuable Citizen.
**Author:** Burstyn, Joan N., Ed.
**Publication Date:** 1996
**Pages:** 229
**Availability:** State University of New York Press, State University Plaza, Albany, NY 12246.

**Abstract:** This collection of essays by various authors discusses the dilemmas that face those who would educate tomorrow's valuable citizens and describes the day-to-day commitment needed to maintain a community. The book gives guidelines for action through examples of current programs that provide a forum for civic discussion and public consensus on the best ways to educate for tomorrow. The 11 essays include: (1) "'What We Call the Beginning Is Often the End'" (Joan N. Burstyn); (2) "Educating for Public and Private Life: Beyond the False Dilemma" (James M. Giarelli; Ellen Giarelli; (3) "Developing the Good Person: The Role of Local Publics" (Thomas Mauhs-Pugh); (4) "To Illuminate or Indoctrinate: Education for Participatory Democracy" (Jerilyn Fay Kelle); (5) "Subverting the Capitalist Model for Education: What Does it Mean to Educate Children to be Valuable Members of a Valuable Society?" (Zeus Yiamouyiannis); (6) "Assaulting the Last Bastions of Authoritarianism: Democratic Education meets Classroom Discipline" (Barbara McEwan); (7) "Practice Makes Perfect: Civic Education by Precept and Example" (Donald Warren); (8) "Preparing Citizens for a Decent Society: Educating for Virtue" (John Covaleskie); (9) "Service Learning as Civic Education: Difference, Culture War, and the Material Basis of a Good Life" (Mary B. Stanley); (10) "Meeting the Demands of Post-modern Society" (Joan N. Burstyn); and (11) "'The End is Where We Start From'" (Joan N. Burstyn).

**ERIC No:** EJ419175
**Title:** Participation in Democratic Citizenship Education.
**Author:** Clark, Todd
**Publication Date:** 1990
**Journal Citation:** Social Studies; v81 p206-09 Sep-Oct 1990
**Abstract:** Argues that school service programs involving students in volunteer community effort should be included in democratic citizenship education. Suggests that encouraging cooperation through volunteer service combats corrosive and anti-democratic effects of excessive individualism. Lists six characteristics of effective programs, compiled by University of Minnesota researchers. Recommends four ways to incorporate service into the social studies curriculum.

**ERIC No:** ED390720
**Title:** Civic Education Through Service Learning. ERIC Digest.
**Author:** Garman, Brian
**Publication Date:** 1995
**Pages:** 2
**Availability:** ERIC Clearinghouse for Social Studies/Social Science Education, 2805 East Tenth Street, Suite 120, Indiana University, Bloomington, IN 47408-2698.
**Abstract:** This digest addresses the decline in the willingness of U.S. youth to participate in service to the community or nation and suggests service learning as a possible remedy for the decline. There are long-term benefits of service learning: (1) helping to build community support for education; (2) facilitating a closer bond between school, community, and home; and (3) endowing students with a sense of civic efficacy and the sense that they can have a positive impact on civic affairs. Suggestions on how to structure an effective service-learning program are provided. Contains eight references.

**ERIC No:** EJ554731
**Title:** Service Learning in Civic Education: A Concept with Long, Sturdy Roots.
**Author:** Hepburn, Mary A.
**Publication Date:** 1997
**Journal Citation:** Theory into Practice; v36 n3 p136-42 Sum 1997
**Abstract:** Service learning in civic education combines in-school learning and out-of-school work to enhance democratic education and assist the community. This paper examines the evolution of service learning through several decades of scholarship in the genre of civic education, citing examples of past notable projects that have linked academic study with the community.

**ERIC No:** EJ540822
**Title:** Meeting the Needs of Middle Level Students through Service Learning.
**Author:** Hope, Warren, C.
**Publication Date:** 1997
**Journal Citation:** NASSP Bulletin; v81 n587 p39-45 Mar 1997
**Abstract:** Service learning is a versatile, developmentally appropriate strategy that integrates public service into student instruction and connects the classroom with the surrounding community and the world. Service learning promotes personal, social, and emotional growth; develops a sense of civic responsibility; provides leadership opportunities; and prepares students for the world of work. This approach is particularly suitable for middle-school students and for curriculum goals. (22 references)

**ERIC No:** EJ554734
**Title:** Community Service in a Multicultural Nation.
**Author:** LeSourd, Sandra J.
**Publication Date:** 1997
**Journal Citation:** Theory into Practice; v36 n3 p157-63 Sum 1997
**Abstract:** Examines human qualities that undergird citizens' commitment to the common good in diverse societies, suggesting that community service fosters such qualities. Planned interactions across social barriers are necessary to develop qualities of citizenship for pluralistic nations.

**Title:** National Evaluation of Learn and Serve America School and Community Based Programs. Final Report.
**Author:** Melchior, Alan
**Publication Date:** 1998
**Where to Obtain this Resource:** Executive summary: <http://heller. brandeis.edu/chr/summary.pdf>; Full report: Corporation for National

Service, 1201 New York Ave NW, Washington DC 20525; Phone: 202-606-5000; URL: <http://www.cns.gov>.

**Abstract:** This report evaluated high quality, Learn and Serve America programs from 1994 to 1997. The evaluation centered on four focus points, short- and long-term participant impacts, services provided to communities, impacts on participating schools, and an analysis of program return on investment. Results showed a positive impact on students immediately after participation, however effects seemed to have dissipated by the follow-up interviews. Student assessment of program experience and service in the community were both ranked very highly.

**ERIC No:** EJ475040
**Title:** The Practice of Citizenship: Learn by Doing.
**Author:** Morse, Suzanne W.
**Publication Date:** 1993
**Journal Citation:** Social Studies; v84 n4 p164-67 Jul-Aug 1993
**Abstract:** Contends that the best way to learn about citizenship is by discussing real societal issues that are connected to student interests. Maintains that a democratic classroom environment also provides an opportunity for practicing civic values. Provides four guidelines for establishing community service projects in the schools.

**ERIC No:** ED396077
**Title:** Serving To Learn, Learning To Serve. Civics and Service from A to Z.
**Author:** Parsons, Cynthia
**Publication Date:** 1996
**Pages:** 108
**Availability:** Corwin Press, Inc., 2455 Teller Road, Thousand Oaks, CA 91320-2218
**Abstract:** This book espouses service learning as an important and integral part of school for students. It stresses the positive benefits to be gained from service learning, as well as the good the activities do for the community. It notes that service learning should be used to promote a sense of civic responsibility and pride in students. It also promotes the intertwining of service and learning as most beneficial to students. The 26 short chapters of the book, based on the letters of the alphabet, cover the following: awards and appreciation; books and birthdays; civics, civility, and concern; daring and doing; equity; French and other foreign languages; government; helping interns; justice; kindness; liability; money; natural science; obligation; physical education; quid pro quo; recreation; SerVermont; time and transportation; United States; value; who; xenophilia; youth; and zeal. Contains 23 resources.

ERIC No: ED403205
Title: Community and Individuality in Civic Education for Democracy.
Author: Patrick, John J.
Publication Date: 1996
Pages: 13
Note: Paper presented at the International Conference on Individualism and Community in a Democratic Society (Washington, DC, October 6-11, 1996).

Abstract: The interactions of individuality and community in a democratic republic have remained the great object of civic inquiries, the perplexing civic problem throughout the more than 200 years of U.S. constitutional history. This paper argues that this inquiry should be at the center of civic education today. Five recommendations for civic educators to meet this challenge include: (1) teach the analysis and appraisal of public issued about community and individuality and emphasize those issues that have been landmarks of public debate in U.S. history; (2) teach comparatively and internationally about public issues pertaining to community and individuality in different constitutional democracies of the world; (3) conduct the classroom and the school in a manner that exemplifies the conjoining of community and individuality in a democratic civic culture; (4) use service learning in the community outside the school to teach civic virtues and skills needed to conjoin community and individuality in civic life; and (5) teach civic knowledge, skills, and virtues that constitute a common core of learning by which to maintain the culture of a community and coterminously teach individuals to think critically for the purposes of freeing themselves from unworthy traditions and to seek improvement of the community.

ERIC No: ED423211
Title: Education for Engagement in Civil Society and Government. ERIC Digest.
Author: Patrick, John J.
Publication Date: 1998
Pages: 2
Availability: ERIC Clearinghouse for Social Studies/Social Science Education, 2805 East Tenth Street, Suite 120, Bloomington, IN 47408.

Abstract: A report by the National Commission on Civic Renewal has sounded alarms about the declining quantity and quality of citizen engagement in U.S. political and civic life. According to the Commission the overall civic condition is weaker than it was and in need of significant improvement. To renew the constructive engagement of citizens in political and civic life intellectual capital must be developed. Intellectual capital is defined as the knowledge of democratic principles and practices and cognitive capacity to apply it to public affairs. The curriculum of schools can be an effective means to development of intellectual capital necessary for constructive civic engagement. Well-designed and delivered courses in civics, government, and U.S. history – based on key ideas, information, and issues of U.S. democracy of the past and present – enable students to acquire a fund of civic/political knowledge that can be called upon to comprehend, cope, and otherwise interact successfully with the issues, problems, and challenges of civil society and government. The curriculum must be anchored in core subjects such as history, geography, civics/government, and economics. Intellectual capital must be combined with social capital in effective education for engagement in political and civic life. The development of social capital can be achieved through experiential learning such as cooperative learning or service learning. Learning experiences that involve cooperation and community service provide opportunities for students to practice skills and behavior that become habits of responsible citizenship. The Digest concludes with a list of eight intellectual and social capital resource organizations for teachers.

**ERIC No:** ED401222
**Title:** Resources on Civic Education for Democracy: International Perspectives. Yearbook No. 1.
**Author:** Patrick, John J., Ed.; Pinhey, Laura A., Ed.
**Publication Date:** 1996
**Pages:** 154
**Availability:** Adjunct ERIC Clearinghouse for International Civic Education, Indiana University, 2805 East Tenth Street, Suite 120, Bloomington, IN 47408-2698; phone: (800) 266-3815; fax: (812) 855-0455.
**Abstract:** This resource guide is intended to facilitate cooperation and exchange of knowledge among civic educators around the world. Divided into four parts, part 1 is a civic education paper, "Principles of Democracy for the Education of Citizens" (John J. Patrick), that discusses facets of the idea of democracy and their relationships to civic education. Part 2 is "An Annotated Bibliography on Civic Education from the ERIC Database"with items selected from 1990 until July 1996 that reflect various projects in the United States and other parts of the world; diverse pedagogical practices; and different levels of education from the primary levels to secondary levels to post-secondary levels. Part 3 includes 15 ERIC Digests on topics in civic education that have been published from 1988-1996. Part 4 is "An International Directory of Civic Education Leaders and Programs" that includes names, addresses, and telephone numbers of prominent persons, projects, and organizations involved in civic educa-

tion from many countries and various regions around the world. The Appendix contains: (1) the CIVITAS brochure; (2) a sample ERIC document resume; (3) a sample ERIC journal article resume; (4) a call for ERIC documents on civic education; (5) an announcement for the ERIC Clearinghouse for Social Studies/Social Science Education book, "Building Civic Education for Democracy in Poland" (Richard C. Remy; Jacek Strzemieczny); and (6) "Civic Education on the Internet: An Introduction to CIVNET."

**ERIC No:** ED415175
**Title:** Resources on Civic Education for Democracy: International Perspectives. Yearbook No. 2.
**Author:** Pinhey, Laura A., Ed.; Boyer, Candace L., Ed.
**Publication Date:** 1997
**Pages:** 198
**Availability:** Adjunct ERIC Clearinghouse for International Civic Education, 2805 East Tenth Street, Suite 120, Bloomington, IN 47408-2698; phone: (800) 266-3815.
**Abstract:** This resource guide is intended to facilitate cooperation and exchange of knowledge among civic educators around the world. The guide is divided into six parts. Part 1 consists of three civic education papers: "Education and Democratic Citizenship: Where We Stand" (Albert Shanker); "Civil Society and Democracy Reconsidered" (Charles Bahmueller); and "Civil Society and the Worldwide Surge of Democracy: Implications for Civic Education" (John J. Patrick). Part 2 features an annotated bibliography of materials about civic education from July 1996 through July 1997 selected from the ERIC database. Part 3 contains nine ERIC Digests on civic education published between 1994 and 1997. Part 4 is an annotated bibliography of books that address key topics about the work of civic educators. Topics covered include comparative politics in democratic societies, Western political philosophy on civil society and democracy, U.S. political/constitutional history, contemporary U.S. civil society, and civic education in the United States. Part 5 is a selective list of Internet resources about international civic education and features information useful to civic educators. Part 6 is an international directory of civic education leaders, programs, organizations, and centers. The entries include names, addresses, telephone numbers, electronic mail addresses, and World Wide Web sites. An appendix concludes the guide and features information about CIVITAS, an International Civic Education Exchange Program and documents and journal articles in the ERIC database.

**ERIC No:** ED413278
**Title:** Service Learning in the Middle School Curriculum: A Resource Book.

**Author:** Schukar, Ron; Johnson, Jacquelyn; Singleton, Laurel R.
**Publication Date:** 1996
**Pages:** 164
**Availability:** Social Science Education Consortium, P.O. Box 21270, Boulder, CO 80301-4270.

**Abstract:** This book incorporates teaching strategies to enhance middle school science and social studies using service learning. The book was developed by teachers who participated in a series of institutes conducted by the Social Science Education Consortium and the Science Discovery Program at the University of Colorado during the summers of 1993 and 1994. Chapters 1 and 2 provide an overview of service learning – what it is, what its benefits are, and how it is related to other current educational reforms, including standards-based education. Chapter 3 introduces the curriculum integration planning framework developed to guide the process of creating integrated science/social studies/service learning units for use in the middle school. Chapter 4 describes several of the integrated units developed in this project, including the two staff-developed demonstration units and six teacher-developed units. A chapter on assessment is included since assessment of integrated units with multiple outcomes is complex. The book concludes with a listing of resources useful to teachers wanting to learn more about service learning.

**Title:** Democratic Education, Student Empowerment, and Community Service: Theory and Practice.
**Authors:** Seigel, Susan, and Virginia Rockwood
**Publication Date:** 1993
**Journal Citation:** Equity and Excellence in Education; v25, p65-70

**Abstract:** The authors define democratic education and argue for a broader definition of democracy, going beyond voting to active participation. They stress the need for democratic experiences within the classrooms to develop social responsibility, and the need for critical thinking skills and contextual information to help students make sense of service experiences. The need for experiential education is also emphasized; a brief review of the major theorists in this area is included. They argue that service-learning must be integrated into the curriculum, not merely tacked on.

**ERIC No:** ED430907
**Title:** Service, Social Studies, and Citizenship: Connections for the New Century. ERIC Digest.
**Author:** Shumer, Robert
**Publication Date:** 1999

**Pages:** 2
**Availability:** ERIC Clearinghouse for Social Studies/Social Science Education, 2805 East Tenth Street, Suite 120, Bloomington, IN 47408; Tel: (800) 266-3815.
**Abstract:** This Digest describes how, by connecting service, social studies, and citizenship, civic educators have the potential to begin the new millennium by initiating a "Century of the Caring Citizen." Effective methods for bringing about the caring citizen are to allow students to learn and develop through active participation in thoughtfully organized experiences that meet actual community needs; to integrate service into students' academic curriculum and provide structured time for thinking, talking, or writing about the service activity; to provide students with opportunities to use nearly acquired skills and knowledge in real-life situations in their own communities; and to enhance what is taught in schools by extending learning into the community and help foster the development of a sense of caring for others. Research indicates that well conceptualized, well-administered service programs produce positive changes in students, including increased social and personal responsibility, more favorable attitudes toward adults, growth in moral and ego development, and increased self-esteem. For social studies teachers to effectively implement service learning, they should be involved in service activities in their preservice training by participating in classrooms where service learning projects are taking place. Existing guidelines on service-learning describe the important components of high-quality programs: (1) provide choice and challenge to students; (2) connect schools and communities in positive ways that meet real needs; and (3) engage in ongoing program assessment and evaluation. Concludes with a list of 12 references.

**Title:** Citizenship Symposium.
**Author:** Skelton, Nan
**Publication Date:** 1993
**Pages:** 29
**Notes:** Conference held September 1, 1993 in Lake Bluff, Illinois.
**Availability:** Lilly Endowment Inc., 28-1 N. Meridian Street, Indianapolis, IN 46208
**Abstract:** These are the proceedings from the Citizenship Symposium held on September 1, 1993. The meeting reflected on public spirit from the 1960's and asked how we can make the national and community service movement a more effective means of civic education and civic leadership development. Sessions included, The Meaning of Citizenship with Nan Skelton and Harry Boyte, The New Environment: National Service with

Susan Stroud, Catherine Milton and Benjamin Barber, Service Training for Civic Education with Tony Massengale, and Closing Reflections with Jon Blyth.

**ERIC No:** EJ554711
**Title:** Community Service Learning and the Social Studies Curriculum: Challenges to Effective Practice.
**Author:** Wade, Rahima C.
**Publication Date:** 1997
**Journal Citation:** Social Studies; v88 n5 p197-202 Sep-Oct 1997
**Abstract:** Discusses some of the cultural and logistical challenges faced by service-learning projects. These challenges include a predisposition toward individualism over collective action, lack of time and emphasis on traditional learning. Provides strategies and approaches for overcoming these challenges. Includes a sample questionnaire for parents and educators.

**ERIC No:** EJ487178
**Title:** Community Service-Learning: Commitment through Active Citizenship.
**Author:** Wade, Rahima C.
**Publication Date:** 1994
**Journal Citation:** Social Studies and the Young Learner; v6 n3 ps1-4 Jan-Feb 1994
**Abstract:** Discusses the history of U.S. community service programs and asserts that the potential benefits for students include increased self-esteem, enhanced motivation and interest in school, improved academic achievement, and increased social responsibility. Includes a list of six curriculum resources and a bibliography.

**ERIC No:** ED395855
**Title:** Service Learning in the Social Studies.
**Publication Date:** 1994
**Pages:** 14
**Availability:** Constitutional Rights Foundation Chicago, 407 South Dearborn, Suite 1700, Chicago, IL 60605.
**Abstract:** This booklet describes the relationship of service learning to the social studies and examines public policy issues as a crucial step in the service learning process. Service learning is defined and explained using the ACT (Active Citizenship Today) approach whereby students: (1) define and focus on their community; (2) research community problems, select one, and research it more fully; (3) analyze and evaluate public policies related to the problem; (4) design and implement a service

project to address the problem; and (5) reflect upon and evaluate the process. Student handouts are included, as well as a resource list for further information.

## 2. Research

**ERIC No:** ED420549
**Title:** Children's Social Consciousness and the Development of Social Responsibility.
**Author:** Berman, Sheldon
**Publication Date:** 1997
**Pages:** 254
**Availability:** State University of New York Press, State University Plaza, Albany, NY 12246; phone: (800) 688-2877.
**Abstract:** This book synthesizes the research in diverse fields of the social studies relating to the development of children's awareness of and responsibility for social inequity and social action. The book addresses the issues concerning: the processes by which young people develop a sense of social responsibility; and classroom and school practices that effectively support this development. The book is divided into six chapters including: (1) "I Care About the World. But I Don't Think It Concerns Me, Even Though It Does."; (2) "The Development of Social Responsibility"; (3) "From Consciousness to Activism"; (4) "Processes that Promote Development"; (5) "Educational Interventions and Social Responsibility"; (6) "The Current State of Educating for Social Responsibility."

**ERIC No:** EJ538439
**Title:** Effects of Participatory Learning Programs in Middle and High School Civic Education.
**Author:** Kim, Simon; And Others
**Publication Date: 1996**
**Journal Citation:** Social Studies; v87 n4 p171-176 Jul-Aug 1996
**Abstract:** Evaluates three participatory civic education learning programs developed by the Citizenship Education Clearinghouse: the Election Program, Missouri State Government Program, and the Metropolitan Issues Program. Evaluation consisted of questionnaires observation, and interviews. Discovers that the programs are both popular and effective.

**ERIC No:** ED415154
**Title:** Engendering Civic Identity through Community Service.
**Author:** Yates, Miranda; Youniss, James
**Publication Date:** 1997

**Pages:** 12
**Note:** Paper presented at the Biennial Meeting of the Society for Research on Child Development (Washington, DC, April 3-6, 1997).

**Abstract:** This paper outlines a theoretical approach to understanding how youth community service participation can stimulate identity development and encourage civic investment. The study elucidates the developmental processes through which individuals become invested in civic activities and the activities in which youth are involved. The paper explains developmental continuity in civic participation from adolescence to adulthood and then illustrates this approach using data from a case study of participants in a school-based service program. Findings are presented from a 1993-1994 juniors' essays on service and from the alumni surveys and essays. Presenting participants' reflections as they go through the program and 3-, 5-, and 10-years later, the study shows how service experience can stimulate reflections on self in relation to society and can foster a sense of agency and responsibility. (Contains 19 references.)

**ERIC No:** ED382358
**Title:** Community Service in Adolescence: Implications for Moral-Political Awareness.
**Author:** Yates, Miranda
**Publication Date:** 1995
**Pages:** 16
**Note:** Paper presented at the Biennial Meeting of the Society for Research in Child Development (61st, Indianapolis, IN, March 30-April 2, 1995).

**Abstract:** This paper provides an overview of research on community service in adolescence and outlines a theoretical approach that relates service participation to identity development. After building the case that the 1990s has been a period of increased interest in the prosocial effects of service participation among school-aged youth, this paper discusses the scope of this interest and describes the current state of the research literature. The report then provides a framework for organizing the literature by delineating three concepts associated with service: agency, which refers to findings that associate service with personal directedness and increased self understanding; social relatedness, which pertains to findings that address the social characteristic of service; and moral-political awareness, which refers to findings that relate service to morality and civic behavior. Taken together, the findings suggest that experiences of service pertain to the process of trying to understand oneself with social-historical reality and helps youth to feel that they can actively "make history," rather than simply "live history," and that service participants come to view themselves as political agents in improving societal conditions. Future directions for developmental research in this area are also discussed.

### 3. Curriculum

**ERIC No:** ED429020
**Title:** VOICE: Violence-Prevention Outcomes in Civic Education. A Program for Elementary Social Studies.
**Authors:** Chilcoat, Kendra Hillman; Farwick, Diane; Eslinger, Mary Vann; Banaszak, Ronald, Sr.
**Publication Date:** 1997
**Pages:** 237
**Abstract:** Violence-Prevention Outcomes in Civic Education (VOICE) is a curriculum program for elementary social studies that incorporates conflict resolution, law-related education, and service learning. These three elements are among those considered to have promise in addressing youth violence. The VOICE curriculum is designed to complement the traditional elementary grade social studies curriculum by helping students develop a deeper understanding of the United States Constitution and the three branches of government. Components of the curriculum include participatory teaching strategies, involvement of outside resource people, conflict resolution skill building, and a service project. The curriculum consists of 50 lessons in seven units of study that have a logical flow; each lesson has teacher directions and student materials for duplication. The units are: (1) "Working Together: Building a Good Foundation in Class"; (2) "Working It Out Together: Mediating Our Conflicts"; (3) "Working Together To Build a Government: Balancing Rights and Safety"; (4) "Working Together To Make Laws: The Legislative Branch"; (5) "Making the Laws Work: The Executive Branch"; (6) "Interpreting the Laws: The Judicial Branch"; and (7) "Taking Action Together: Service and Learning." The curriculum fulfills the government goals of fifth-grade social studies and supplements a typical fifth-grade U.S. history textbook. An appendix contains 6 different sample assessment tools.

**Title:** Active Citizenship Today Field Guide [High School and Middle School Editions].
**Author:** Close Up Foundation and Constitutional Rights Foundation
**Publication Date:** 1994
**Pages:** 196
**Availability:** Close Up Foundation, 44 Canal Center Plaza, Alexandria, VA 22314-1592; Phone: (703) 706-3640; Email: <cup@closeup.org>; URL:

http://www.closeup.org/>; or Constitutional Rights Foundation, 601 South Kingsley Drive, Los Angeles, CA 90005; Phone: (213) 487-5590; Email: <crfcitizen@aol.com>; URL: <www.crf-usa.org>.

**Abstract:** Written for middle school and high school youth, these citizenship manuals guide students in learning about their community and exploring how they can help to change it. This process includes examining the past, present, and future community; identifying problems; searching for solutions; exploring options; and taking action. Activities include research, public relations, community resources, public speaking, persuasive writing, government process, planning, conducting meetings, fund raising, resolving group conflict evaluation, and reflection. An evaluation questionnaire is included as well as a directory of supporting organizations. Teacher's guides are also available.

**ERIC No:** ED424166
**Title:** Adventures in Law and History. Volume I: Native Americans, the Spanish Frontier, and the Gold Rush. A Law and Civic Education Curriculum for Upper Elementary Grades with Units on Rules and Laws, Property, and Authority.
**Author:** Croddy, Marshall; Degelman, Charles; Doggett, Keri; Hayes, Bill
**Publication Date:** 1997
**Pages:** 104
**Availability:** Constitutional Rights Foundation, Publication Orders Department, 601 S. Kingsley Drive, Los Angeles, CA 90005; tel: (213) 487-5590; fax: (213) 386-0459; Web site: www.erf.usa.org>.

**Abstract:** This is volume one of a two-volume civics curriculum on law and effective citizenship for upper-elementary students. The lessons, set in American historical eras, engage students in cooperative-learning activities, role plays, simulations, readers theater, stories, and guided discussions, which introduce and reinforce law-related and civic education concepts and skills. Designed to meet the needs of a multi-centered student population, this curriculum features step-by-step teaching procedures, reproducible worksheet and activity masters, lessons linking the historical and law-related content to the present, and service-learning opportunities. This volume contains 3 units and 18 lessons in total. In unit 1, "Rules and Laws," students visit a Native American Chumash village and discover how rules and laws derived from myth and tradition help the Indians govern tribal life and resolve conflict. In unit 2, "Property," students meet Luisa, a girl living in a pueblo on the California Spanish frontier in the early 19th century. Students explore the concept of property and how law helps resolve conflicts over property. In unit 3, "Authority," students experience a hypothetical mining camp in California's Gold

Rush era and discover what life might be like without effective authority. Students also examine executive, legislature, and judiciary roles.

**ERIC No:** ED424167
**Title:** Adventures in Law and History. Volume II: Coming to America, Colonial America, and the Revolutionary Era. A Law and Civic Education Curriculum for Upper Elementary Grades with Units on Equal Protection, Due Process, Authority, and Rights and Responsibilities.
**Author:** Croddy, Marshall; Degelman, Charles; Doggett, Keri; Hayes, Bill
**Publication Date:** 1997
**Pages:** 145
**Availability:** Constitutional Rights Foundation, Publication Orders Department, 601 S. Kingsley Drive, Los Angeles, CA 90005; Tel: (213) 487-5590; Fax: (213) 386-0459; Web site: <www.crf-usa.org>.
**Abstract:** This is volume two of a two-volume civics curriculum on law and effective citizenship for upper-elementary students. The lessons, set in American historical eras, engage students in cooperative-learning activities, role plays, simulations, readers theater, stories, and guided discussions, which introduce and reinforce law-related and civic education concepts and skills. Designed to meet the needs of a multi-centered student population, this curriculum features step-by-step teaching procedures, reproducible worksheet and activity masters, lessons linking the historical and law-related content to the present, and service-learning opportunities. This volume contains four units and 21 lessons in total. In unit 1, "Immigration, Diversity, and Equal Protection," students use the methods of historiography to trace the immigrant origins of five families whose ancestors came to America seeking opportunity and freedom and struggled for equality. In unit 2, "Due Process," students visit a hypothetical New England village of the colonial era and learn essential lessons about due process. In unit 3, "Authority," students explore the concepts of authority by helping a tired king rule his kingdom and view the causes of the American Revolution through the eyes of Bostonians as the colonies moved toward independence. In unit 4, "Rights and Responsibilities," students learn about the rights and responsibilities of citizenship by helping James Madison draft the Bill of Rights and also about the appropriate limits of those rights. As a conclusion, students create their own Bill of Rights and Responsibilities.

**Title:** City Youth Student Workbook: Education and Community Action.
**Authors:** Croddy, Marshall; Keri Doggett
**Publication Date:** 1995
**Notes:** Use in conjunction with "City Youth Teacher Guide".

**Availability:** Constitutional Rights Foundation, 601 S. Kingsley Dr., Los Angeles, CA 90005; Phone: (213) 487-5590; Email: <crf@crf-usa.org>; URL: <www.crf-usa.org>.

**Abstract:** This is a student workbook that leads students through service-learning and civic centered lessons. It helps students to define their community in terms of their own lives, to analyze community needs, to learn problem-solving skills, and to participate in action projects designed to affect change in their own schools and communities.

**ERIC No:** ED431685
**Title:** Teaching Presidential Elections. A Social Studies/Service Learning Teaching Unit for the Middle Grades.
**Author:** Greco, Lisa M.
**Publication Date:** 1997
**Pages:** 27
**Abstract:** This curriculum unit on social studies and service learning was developed during the 1996 Presidential elections. In this unit middle school students not only learn about citizenship and democracy, they also practice civic action through voter registration and community surveying. The unit helps students develop critical thinking skills as they become active members of their own communities, and causes them to reevaluate the leadership potential of youth. The unit provides an overview that includes objectives, key terms, and an outline of the 8 part unit: (1) "Introduction"; (2) "History Behind the Vote"; (3) "The Nominating Process"; (4) "Electoral vs. Popular"; (5) "Key Campaign Issues"; (6) "Factors That Influence the Election Process"; (7) "Who Should Be President?"; and (8) "Impact of the Elections." Each unit offers student assignments and activities. Appended are a sample student survey on political issues, a sample mock election ballot, and a presidential debates evaluation form.

**ERIC No:** ED340654
**Title:** Civitas: A Framework for Civic Education.
**Author:** Quigley, Charles N., Ed.; Bahmueller, Charles, Ed.
**Publication Date:** 1991
**Pages:** 693
**Availability:** NCSS Publications, c/o Maxway Data Corp., Suite 1105, 225 West 34th Street, New York, NY 10001.
**Abstract:** CIVITAS is a curriculum framework that sets forth a set of national goals to be achieved in a civic education curriculum, primarily for K-12 public and private schools. It is a framework that proposes to specify the knowledge and skills needed by citizens to perform their roles in U.S. democracy. There are two major sections in the framework. It

begins with a rationale that explains the basic philosophy, purpose and nature of the framework. The other major section is a statement of goals and objectives that civic education should foster. This section is divided into three parts – (1) Civic Virtue, (2) Civic Participation, and (3) Civic Knowledge and Intellectual Skills. Parts 2 and 3 contain model scope and sequence statements that suggest what aspects of the subjects in the framework can be taught at varying school grades and how they may be taught. The part on Civic Knowledge and Intellectual Skills comprises by far the largest portion of the framework. It organizes summaries of numerous topics into three main groupings: the nature of politics and government; public government in the United States; and the role of the citizen. The intended audience for the curriculum is educators at state and local levels concerned with the development of civic education curricula in the schools. Classroom teachers also may find the framework a useful resource and reference book. A six page executive summary is appended.

**ERIC No:** EJ548164
**Title:** Lessons Based on a Service-Learning Framework.
**Publication Date:** 1997
**Journal Citation:** Social Studies Review; v36 n2 p15-25 Spr-Sum 1997
**Abstract:** Presents six service learning lesson plans from the Constitutional Rights Foundation. Each lesson plan represents a step in a larger service project. The plans include "Defining and Assessing Your Community"; "Choosing and Researching a Problem"; "Examining Policy"; "Exploring Options"; and "Taking Action." Includes instructional materials and handouts.

**ERIC No:** EJ548174
**Title:** Resources.
**Publication Date:** 1997
**Journal Citation:** Social Studies Review; v36 n2 p54-56 Spr-Sum 1997
**Abstract:** Briefly describes resources that educators and students can use to design service-learning projects. These resources include free materials, books, web sites, information on grants, videos, journals, and organizations. The resources cover a broad range of approaches, projects, and methods.

*4. Program Examples*

**ERIC No:** EJ558937
**Title:** Public Life: A Contribution to Democratic Education.
**Author:** Kaplan, Andrew

**Publication Date:** 1997
**Journal Citation:** Journal of Curriculum Studies; v29 n4 p431-53 Jul-Aug 1997
**Abstract:** Describes an experimental course at an urban school that focuses on experiences of service work outside the school as well as involvement in the political and social structure within the school. Suggests ways that schools can design a curriculum that reflects on social activity as an element of community life.

**ERIC No:** EJ538161
**Title:** Service Learning: Making A Difference in the Community.
**Author:** McPherson, Kate
**Publication Date:** 1997
**Journal Citation:** Schools in the Middle; v6 n3 p9-15 Jan-Feb 1997
**Abstract:** Describes six community-based service-learning projects that are available to students as an alternative learning environment. Presents goals of service learning, including academic development, civic responsibility, personal development, social responsibility, career development, and ethical development. Discusses research indicating that participation has positive effects on student's personal development, and offers suggestions for service activities and for maximizing the potential for service learning.

**ERIC No:** EJ522267
**Title:** Youth Citizenship Awards Program. Teaching Strategy.
**Author:** Minkler, John
**Publication Date:** 1996
**Journal Citation:** Update on Law-Related Education; v20 n1 p20-22 Win 1996
**Abstract:** Describes a service-learning project where students identify a real political problem, research related issues, and propose a solution. Members of the U.S. Congress and county offices of education have created corresponding awards programs. Includes procedures for creating a local project.

**ERIC No:** ED431672
**Title:** Education for Citizenship: Ideas and Innovations in Political Learning.
**Author:** Reeher, Grant, Ed.; Cammarano, Joseph, Ed.
**Publication Date:** 1997
**Pages:** 248
**Availability:** Rowman & Littlefield Publishers, Inc., Order Dept., 15200

NBN Way, P.O. Box 191, Blue Ridge Summit, PA 17214; Tel: (800) 462-6420 (Toll Free).

**Abstract:** These essays address education for citizenship at a specific, concrete level. The collection offers examples of efforts to create among students a new set of what Alexis de Tocqueville called "mores" or culturally defining "habits of the heart" that enhance citizenship, foster a sense of connectedness to a community, and support the practices, basic values, and institutions necessary for the democratic process. An introduction entitled "Some Themes from Recent Innovations and Questions for the Future" is given. The 13 essays following the introduction are: (1) "Teaching American Politics through Service: Reflections on a Pedagogical Strategy" (Craig A. Rimmerman); (2) "Service Learning as Civic Learning: Lessons We Can Learn from Our Students" (Richard M. Battistoni); (3) "The Urban Agenda Project" (Otto Feinstein; James D. Chesney); (4) "Citizenship Courses as Life-Changing Experiences" (William D. Coplin); (5) "Public Affairs Internships: Coming of Age" (Glen A. Halva-Neubauer); (6) "Enhancing Citizenship through Active Learning: Simulations on the Policy Process" (Joseph Cammarano; Linda L. Fowler); (7) "Doing the Rights Thing: Tales of Citizenship and Free Speech" (Marc Lendler); (8) "Teaching the Art of Public Deliberation: National Issues Forums on Campus" (Daniel W. O'Connell); (9) "Democratizing the Classroom: The Individual Learning Contract" (John F. Freie)' (10) "Wading in the Deep: Supporting Emergent Anarchies" (Naeem Inayatullah); (11) "Teaching Deliberation: Citizenship Education and Cross-Disciplinary Team Teaching" (Mark Rupert); (12) "Using the Internet to Enhance Classroom and Citizenship Information" (William Ball); and (13) "The Internet as a Tool for Student Citizenship" (Kimberley P. Canfield).

**ERIC No:** ED421406
**Title:** Social Issues and Service at the Middle Level.
**Author:** Totten, Samuel, Ed.; Pedersen, Jon E., Ed.
**Publication Date:** 1997
**Pages:** 378
**Availability:** Allyn & Bacon, Simon & Schuster Education Group, 160 Gould Street, Needham Heights, MA 02494 (Order No. H-5093-3).
**Abstract:** This book provides a powerful and clear picture of some of the outstanding programs designed and implemented in the United States to provide young adolescents with rich, meaningful, and powerful learning activities with community service. The book is comprised of two parts with 18 essays and an introduction. The essays reflect a range of experience. Part 1, "Social Issues," includes: (1) "Social Issues in the Middle

School Curriculum: Retrospect and Prospect" (James A. Beane); (2) "Challenging Barriers: A Unit in Developing an Awareness and Appreciation for Differences in Individuals with Physical and Mental Challenges" (Pauline S. Chandler); (3) "Implementing an Interdisciplinary Unit on the Holocaust" (Regina Townsend; William G. Wraga); (4) "The Homeless: An Issue-Based Interdisciplinary Unit in an Eighth Grade Class" (Belinda Y. Louie; Douglas H. Louie; Margaret Heras); (5) "Making Plays, Making Meaning, Making Change" (Kathy Greeley); (6) "Teleconversing about Community Concerns and Social Issues" (Judith H. Vesel); (7) "Using Telecommunications to Nurture the Global Village" (Dell Salza); (8) "New Horizons for Civic Education: A Multidisciplinary Social Issues Approach for Middle Schools" (Ronald A. Banaszak; H. Michael Hartoonian; James S. Leming); and (9) "Future Problem Solving: Preparing Middle School Students to Solve Community Problems" (Richard L. Kurtzberg; Kristin Faughnan). Part 2, "Service," contains: (1) "Alienation or Engagement? Service Learning May Be an Answer" (Joan Schine; Alice Halsted); (2) "Service Learning: A Catalyst for Social Action and School Change at the Middle Level" (Wokie Weah; Madeleine Wegner); (3) "The Community as Classroom: Service Learning at the Lewis Armstrong Middle School" (Ivy Diton; Mary Ellen Levin); (4) "Incorporating Service Learning into the School Day" (Julie Ayers; Kathleen Kennedy Townsend); (5) "Science Technology-Society: An Approach to Attaining Student Involvement in Community Action Projects" (Curt Jeffryes; Robert E. Yager; Janice Conover); (6) "Calling Students to Action: How Wayland Middle School Puts Theory into Practice" (Stephen Feinberg; Richard Schaye; David Summergrad); (7) "Our Forest, Their Forest: A Program That Stimulates Long-Term Learning and Community Action" (Patricia McFarlane Soto; John H. Parker; George E. O'Brien); (8) "Every Step Counts: Service and Social Responsibility" (Larry Dieringer; Esther Weisman Kattef); and (9) "The Letter that Never Arrived: The Evolution of a Social Concerns Program in a Middle School" (Robyn L. Morgan; Robert W. Moderhak).

## 5. Organizations

**American Political Science Association**
1527 New Hampshire Avenue, NW
Washington, DC 20036-1206
Phone: (202) 483-2512; Fax: (202) 483-2657
Email: <apsa@apsanet.org>
The American Political Science Association has resources and references and links to other organizations working on teaching, civic education, and service learning on its web site, as follows:

Teaching and Learning Politics, Government and Public Policy:
<www.apsanet.org/teach/index.cfm>
Civic Education
<www.apsanet.org/CENnet/>
Service Learning
<www.apsanet.org/service/>

### Center for Civic Education
5146 Douglas Fir Rd., Calabasas, CA 91302-1467
Phone: (818) 591-9321; Fax: (818) 591-9330
Email: <cce@civiced.org>; URL: <http://www.civiced.org/>
The Center for Civic Education is a nonprofit, nonpartisan educational corporation dedicated to fostering the development of informed, responsible participation in civic life by citizens committed to values and principles fundamental to American constitutional democracy.

### Center for Democracy and Citizenship
Humphrey Institute of Public Affairs, University of Minnesota, Twin Cities Campus
301 19th Avenue South, Minneapolis, MN 55455
Phone: (612) 625-0142; Fax: (612) 625-3513
Email: cdcweb@hhh.umn.edu; URL: http://www.hhh.umn.edu/centers/cdc/
The mission of the Center for Democracy and Citizenship is the promotion of democracy and the strengthening of citizenship and civic education within a variety of settings, with a special emphasis on youth.

### Civic Practices Network
Center for Human Resources, Heller School for Advanced Studies in Social Welfare
Brandeis University, 60 Turner Street, Waltham, MA 02154
Phone: (617) 736-4890; Email: <cpn@tiac.net>; URL: <http://www.cpn. org>
CPN is a collaborative and nonpartisan project bringing together a diverse array of organizations and perspectives within a new citizenship movement. CPN is designed to bring schooling for active citizenship, which has always been at the heart of our rich democratic and associational life, into the information age.

### Civnet
<http://civnet.org/index.htm.>
Civnet, published by CIVITAS, is a Web site for civic education practitioners (teachers, teacher trainers, curriculum designers), as well as schol-

ars, policymakers, civic-minded journalists, and non-governmental organizations (NGOs) promoting civil society all over the world. Civnet includes textbooks, lesson plans, original journal articles and book reviews, civic news headlines, events listings, organizational contacts, and a lot more.

## Close Up Foundation

44 Canal Center Plaza, Alexandria, VA 22314
Phone: (800) 256-7387 or (703) 706-3300; Fax: (703) 706-0001
URL: <http://www.closeup.org>; Email: <service.learning@closeup.org>
The mission of the Close Up Foundation is to help citizens become responsible participants in the democratic process. The Foundation is committed to providing educational programs in government and citizenship for young people, teachers and other adults so that citizens of all ages might gain a practical understanding of how public policy affects their lives and how individual and collective efforts affect public policy.

## Constitutional Rights Foundation

601 South Kingsley Drive, Los Angeles, CA 90005
Phone: (213) 487-5590; Fax: (213) 386-0459
Email: <crfcitizen@aol.com>; URL: <http://www.crf-usa.org>
Constitutional Rights Foundation seeks to instill in our nation's youth a deeper understanding of citizenship through values expressed in our Constitution and its Bill of Rights, and educate them to become active and responsible participants in our society.

## Education for Democracy/International (ED/I)

American Federation of Teachers, International Affairs Department
555 New Jersey Avenue, N.W., Washington, D.C. 20001-2079
Phone: (202) 393-7484; Fax: (202) 879-4502
Email: <iadaft@aol.com>; URL: <http://civnet.org/civitas.edi.htm>
The ED/I project focuses its resources on promoting educational activities that improve the teaching of democracy and civics throughout the world. The project has three main activities: teacher training and curriculum development, democratic skills and leadership training, and publications on democracy and education.

## ERIC Clearinghouse for Social Studies/Social Science Education

2805 East Tenth Street, Suite 120, Bloomington, IN 47408-2698
Phone: (812) 855-3838; Toll-free/TDD: (800) 266-3815; Fax: (812) 855-0455
Email: <ericso@indiana.edu>; URL: <http://www.indiana.edu/~ssdc/eric_chess.htm>

ERIC/ChESS serves teachers, parents, administrators, policymakers, researchers, students, and anyone else interested in information on social studies and social science education. ERIC/ChESS is home to three adjunct ERIC clearinghouses: Adjunct ERIC Clearinghouse for U.S.-Japan Studies; Adjunct ERIC Clearinghouse for International Civic Education; and the Adjunct ERIC Clearinghouse for Service-Learning. Since 1986, ERIC/ChESS has been located within the Social Studies Development Center of Indiana University.

**Learn and Serve America Exchange**
Phone: (877)572-3924 (toll-free); URL: <http://www.lsaexchange.org>
The Learn and Serve America Exchange, led by the National Youth Leadership Council supports service-learning programs in schools, colleges and universities, and community organizations across the country through peer-based training and technical assistance. If you need assistance implementing service-learning programs, have questions, or simply want to speak with someone who has "been there," you can utilize the Exchange as a resource.

**Learn and Serve America National Service-Learning Clearinghouse**
University of Minnesota, 1954 Buford Avenue
R-460 VoTech Building, St. Paul, MN 55108-6197
Phone: (800) 808-7378, or (612) 625-6276; Fax: (612) 625-6277
Email: <serve@tc.umn.edu>; URL: <http://umn.edu/~serve>
The Learn and Serve America National Service-Learning Clearinghouse is a comprehensive information system that focuses on all dimensions of service learning, covering kindergarten through higher education (school-based), as well as community-based initiatives. The center of the Clearinghouse Consortium is located at the University of Minnesota, with assistance from thirteen other institutions and organizations.

**National Alliance for Civic Education (NACE)**
University of Maryland
Room 3111
Van Munching Hall
College Park, Maryland 20742
Phone: (301) 405-4753
Fax: (301) 314-9346
Email: <CL26@umail.umd.edu>
The American Political Science Association has joined with over 80 group and individual charter members, including the National Council for the Social Studies, the American Federation of Teachers, the National Confer-

ence of State Legislators and Campus Compact in a coalition to respond to the need to assure that youth and young adults acquire the knowledge, skills and practical experience needed to become active and informed participants in civic life and public affairs. NACE currently invites endorsements and participation from more educational groups, faculty and teachers. The coordinating charter member of NACE is William A. Galston, University of Maryland School of Public Affairs. Sheilah Mann, Director of Education and Professional Affairs at APSA will serve as the Association's liaison with NACE.

### National Council for the Social Studies
3501 Newark Street, NW, Washington, DC 20016
Phone: (202) 966-7840; Email: <webmaster@ncss.org>; URL: <http://www.ncss.org>
NCSS is the largest association in the country devoted solely to social studies education. NCSS engages and supports educators in strengthening and advocating social studies.

### National Helpers Network, Inc.
875 Sixth Ave., Suite 206, New York, NY 10001
Phone: (212) 679-2482; Fax: (212) 679-7461
Email: <info@nationalhelpers.org>; URL: <www.nationalhelpers.org>
As a national leader in the service learning movement, the National Helpers Network provides expert training, assistance and on-site guidance to schools and youth serving agencies around the country.

# Appendix B

## APSA Task Force
## on Civic Education

In the Fall of 1996, the American Political Science Association established the Task Force on Civic Education to initiate a civic education program in political science that focuses on:

- Research and Communication as a means of encouraging new research, examining current research and disseminating conclusions drawn regarding civic trust, engagement and education;
- References and Guides that compile papers addressing civic trust and participation; and
- Workshops and Short Courses as forums for sharing and exchanging ideas regarding student cynicism while also encouraging participation.

The Task Force will achieve these goals by strategically addressing its mission, which reinforces its objectives of:

- Providing clear and analytic descriptions of the current trend toward "civic disengagement" from the political process;
- Providing evidence regarding the failure to politically educate students in the craft and practices of the "political machine";
- Articulating strategies for educators to utilize in teaching the craft and practices of politics.

Task Force Members:
Melvin Dubnick, Rutgers University, cochair
Jean Bethke Elshtain, University of Chicago, cochair
Richard Brody, Stanford University
Lief Carter, Colorado College
Mary A. Hepburn, University of Georgia
Margaret Levi, University of Washington

Susan A. MacManus, University of South Florida
Richard G. Neimi, University of Rochester
Ronald J. Oakerson, Houghton College
Robert D. Putnam, Harvard University
Wendy M. Rahn, University of Minnesota
Alan Rosenthal, Rutgers University
Edward Thompson, III, California State University, San Marcos
M. Kent Jennings, University of California, Santa Barbara, 1998-99 APSA
    President
Elinor Ostrom, Indiana University, 1997-98, APSA President

# Appendix C

## Articulation Statement: A Call for Reactions and Contributions

*APSA Task Force on Civic Education*

### Brief Task Force History

In 1996 Lin Ostrom, APSA president-elect, organized the Task Force and arranged funding for a mission lasting up to seven years. The Task Force held a three-day retreat in March of 1997 and has met in shorter sessions several times since. We regularly exchange ideas on an in-house chat list. Our Statement of Purpose, initially drafted at the retreat, was published in the December, 1997, *PS: Political Science and Politics*, page 745.

### The Problem

We start with the evidence suggesting mounting political apathy in the United States. We see it in long and short time-series studies of such things as voter turnout and student interest in politics. The Task Force is actively examining the various research findings that may explain the dimensions of this presumably multi-faceted problem. Long-term efforts to reverse these trends must obviously address many possible causes. We do, however, take as axiomatic that current levels of political knowledge, political engagement, and political enthusiasm are so low as to threaten the vitality and stability of democratic politics in the United States. We believe political education in the United States is inadequate across the board. We believe that we who have chosen to teach politics as our profession bear major responsibility for addressing the problem.

### The Discussion

Last December, Task Force members took part in the following in-house survey. Each of us was asked to respond to the following item: State in one or two sentences what you believe to be the most important single civic lesson that members of a participatory democracy must learn in order to play effective and responsible civic roles. Twelve members responded. The twelve responses, on first viewing, ranged widely. They included such phrases as:

- "learning to lose gracefully"
- "know that democracy is an ongoing and very much unfinished drama about the struggle to make peace"
- "capacity to access and critically assess governance-related and issue-relevant information"
- "why we must have rule of law"
- "tolerance of diverse opinions"
- "the efficacy of collaboration"
- "exposing students to central and political traditions of the nation"
- "play up the dignity and standing of the category 'citizen'"

Our discussions of the responses produced agreement with Bob Putnam's reduction of the responses to the following categories:

Teach tolerance
Teach collaboration
Teach analysis
Teach our traditions

These four responses may indeed reduce to one: Teach the motivation and competence to engage actively in public problem-solving.

We would like to know how you would respond to our one-item survey question. However, we are even more interested in your reactions to one striking implication of our initial responses and these codings of them. The implication is that teaching "about government" will not itself provide the political education we need. The thrust of many of our in-house responses suggested two new and we think complimentary directions that political education should take: (1) The importance of teaching the liberal aspirations to freedom, dignity, and equality embedded in our political history and traditions; (2) The importance of learning the practical wisdom necessary to be a competent and hopeful political actor in all social settings, many of which, e.g., corporate management, labor union organization and church governance, have no necessary connection to the affairs of national, state, and local government.

Both of these directions, if we take them seriously, imply a major reexamination of political education throughout the U.S., both in the undergraduate and in the K-12 curricula. To do so would have, as the cliche puts it, "vast consequences" for the discipline's approach to the roles its members play as civic educators. Many of us on the task force have come to see that our disciplinary emphasis on "value neutrality" must be adjusted in the civic education classroom to reflect the need to promote and enhance basic democratic values. Our reliance on "critical thinking," without a moral framework with which to think critically, may be part of the problem. It may feed not healthy skepticism but unhealthy cynicism and political disengagement.

Virtually every other academic discipline implicitly claims to teach its students substantive knowledge that is valuable and good. We do not by any means reject teaching the facts of political life. Recent findings suggest that active political participation correlates positively with factual knowledge about governmental and political practices. The call to "teach our traditions"is not a call to return to historical, and often oppressive and exclusionary practices. Nor is the call to "teach tolerance" an innocuous call to "teach values." Tolerance, as both ancient and contemporary political experience shows, seems one of the most difficult of all political achievements. This very difficulty leads us to believe that we must specifically teach tolerance, and the specific political virtues we associate with tolerance, if we are to teach politics as the practice of competent and effective problem-solving in human groups.

In sum, we believe that the factual political knowledge we do and must teach can only become meaningful in political practice when presented within a valuational framework. We believe we must therefore teach the specific virtues on which effective political practice depends. We believe we must unequivocally teach the value of democratic aspirations to human liberation and human dignity. Without this framework, our descriptions of political facts and political virtues will not inspire and motivate people to the level of civic engagement that a healthy democratic polity requires.

# Appendix D

## Declaration of the National Alliance for Civic Education

The recently released NAEP Report on the 1998 Civic Education Assessment indicates widespread deficiencies in the civic knowledge of U.S. students. Other recent studies document the diminished engagement of young Americans in our nation's public life.

No single institution bears sole responsibility for this problem. But we believe that educational institutions can make a key contribution to solving it. There is persuasive evidence that rigorous and multifaceted civic education in schools, primary and secondary, can improve students' knowledge, and that this knowledge promotes civic beliefs, civic character, and civic involvement. There is also evidence that other key programs and practices – such as a democratic school climate, the regular reading of newspapers, training in voting, mock conventions, student contact with public officials, and school and community-based service learning – can boost civic knowledge and skills.

Many individuals and groups have worked for years to further the cause of civic education. We believe that the time has come to band together to achieve greater visibility, efficacy, and mutual reinforcement. To this end, we the undersigned are coming together to form the National Alliance for Civic Education. We urge all like-minded individuals and organizations to join us.

The goals of this coalition are:

To raise the amount, quality, and visibility of civic education in the school curriculum;

To dramatically increase high-quality pre-service and in-service training opportunities for teachers involved in civic education;

To provide teachers with improved access to reliable information on curricula, texts, materials; and pedagogical practices that effectively engage students in civic learning;

To offer students expanded opportunities to participate meaningfully in the civic life of their communities;

To intensify community support for civic education initiatives, including parents, youth organizations, community groups, and the media;

To mobilize institutions of higher education on behalf of civic education, especially the training of teachers involved in civic education;

To encourage every state to include rigorous programs of civic education in schools and to systematically assess their effectiveness; and

To encourage the federal government to administer the NAEP Civics Assessment more frequently and with state-level results to make it more useful for improving state and local civic education programs.

Beyond these specific goals, the Alliance will work to help citizens across the country better understand the significance of effective civic education for a well-functioning democracy. Our nation's civic vitality and its democratic future are at stake.

For further information contact: National Alliance for Civic Education, University of Maryland, Room 3111, Van Munching Hall, College Park, MD 20742, Phone: (301) 405-4753 Fax: (301) 314-9346 E-mail: <CL26@umail.umd.edu>. To find a list of the organizations and individuals endorsing the National Alliance for Civic Education when it was launched in May 2000, see <www.apsanet.org/teach/nace.cfm>.

# Contributors

*Herbert M. Atherton* is Director of Domestic Programs at the Center for Civic Education in Calabasas, California.

*Richard M. Battistoni* is a Professor of Political Science at Providence College.

*Stephen Earl Bennett* is Professor of Political Science at the University of Cincinnati.

*Harry C. Boyte* is Co-Director of the Center for Democratic Citizenship of the Humphrey Institute for Public Affairs and Senior Fellow and Member of the Graduate Faculty of the College of Arts and Sciences at the University of Minnesota.

*Steven Chaffee* is a Professor in the Department of Communication at the University of California, Santa Barbara, where he also holds the Arthur N. Rupe Chair in Social Effects of Mass Communication.

*Jan Goehring* is Program Principal of the National Conference of State Legislatures in Denver, CO.

*Mary A. Hepburn* is a Professor Emerita, Social Science Education, and was head of the Citizen Education Division of the Carl Venson Institute of Government, University of Georgia.

*Karl Kurtz* is Director of the Trust for Representative Democracy of the National Conference of State Legislatures in Denver, CO.

*Frank H. Mackaman* is Executive Director of the Dirksen Congressional Center in Pekin, Illinois.

*Susan MacManus* is a Professor of Government and International Affairs at the University of South Florida in Tampa.

*Sheilah Mann* is Director of Education and Professional Development at the American Political Science Association in Washington, DC.

*John J. Patrick* is a Professor at the Indiana University School of Education in Bloomington, where he also is Director of the Social Studies Development Center and Director of the ERIC Clearinghouse for Social Studies/Social Science Education at Indiana University.

*Iara Peng* is a Senior Research Associate at Doble Research Associates in Englewood Cliffs, New Jersey.

*Alan Rosenthal* is a Professor of Political Science at Rutgers University in New Brunswick, New Jersey, where he also is an associate of the Eagleton Institute of Politics.

175

*Andrea Roufs* is an information specialist of the National Service-Learning Clearinghouse at the University of Minnesota, St. Paul.

*Andrea Schade* is an associate of the Dirksen Congressional Center in Pekin, Illinois.

*Rob Shumer* is Director of the National Service-Learning Clearinghouse at the University of Minnesota, St. Paul.

*John G. Stone III* is a retired career executive of the District of Columbia government. Representing the American Society for Public Administration (ASPA), he helped establish the public service academy at Anacostia High School in the District of Columbia, where he is chairperson of the academy steering committee.

*Ann Treacy* is an information specialist of the National Service-Learning Clearinghouse at the University of Minnesota, St. Paul.